"I have worked with this curriculum for more than a decade. I have seen the Spirit of God use this material to lead to the kind of spiritual reflection that encourages spiritual growth and draws one closer to God. I am certain it will be a spiritual catalyst for your group."

—DARRELL BOCK
research professor of New Testament Studies, professor of Spiritual Development and Culture, Dallas Theological Seminary

"The TRANSFORMING LIFE series involves spiritual formation elements that are individual and community-based, reflective and active—all working together in their proper time and manner. It is both scriptural and reality-based in unique and life-changing ways."

—BRAD SMITH
president, Bakke Graduate University

"An outstanding tool in the development of men and women of faith! I have personally used the principles and concepts of the earlier versions of this material for the past eight years; I can assure you that it is a time-tested, invaluable resource that I look forward to using in the years to come."

—DAN BOSCO
community life pastor, Vail Bible Church, Avon, Colorado

COMMUNITY

Discovering Who We Are Together

Center for Christian Leadership at Dallas Theological Seminary

NAVPRESS®

BRINGING TRUTH TO LIFE

The Navigators is an international Christian organization. Our mission is to reach, disciple, and equip people to know Christ and to make Him known through successive generations. We envision multitudes of diverse people in the United States and every other nation who have a passionate love for Christ, live a lifestyle of sharing Christ's love, and multiply spiritual laborers among those without Christ.

NavPress is the publishing ministry of The Navigators. NavPress publications help believers learn biblical truth and apply what they learn to their lives and ministries. Our mission is to stimulate spiritual formation among our readers.

© 2004 by Center for Christian Leadership

ISBN 1-57683-559-6

Cover design by Arvid Wallen
Creative Team: Jay Howver, Karen Lee-Thorp, Cara Iverson, Glynese Northam

Some of the anecdotal illustrations in this book are true to life and are included with the permission of the persons involved. All other illustrations are composites of real situations, and any resemblance to people living or dead is coincidental.

Unless otherwise identified, all Scripture quotations in this publication are taken from the HOLY BIBLE: NEW INTERNATIONAL VERSION® (NIV®). Copyright © 1973, 1978, 1984 by International Bible Society. Used by permission of Zondervan Publishing House. All rights reserved.

Printed in Canada

1 2 3 4 5 6 7 8 9 10 / 08 07 06 05 04

Table of Contents

Acknowledgments

The TRANSFORMING LIFE series is based on a curriculum developed at Dallas Theological Seminary for its Spiritual Formation program, under the guidance of the Center for Christian Leadership. Hundreds of seminary students have benefited from this material, and now this adapted version makes it available to local churches and ministries.

This series would not have been possible without the contributions of many people and the support of Dallas Theological Seminary. The person primarily responsible for this series is Erik Petrik, senior pastor at Vail Bible Church in Vail, Colorado. As the director of the Spiritual Formation program in the late 1990s through 2000, Erik and his team developed the philosophy of this series and its fundamental components. The team he gathered included men and women with great spiritual insight and extensive ministry experience. It was primarily due to Erik's vision and the team's refining, researching, and writing that this series came to life.

In addition, the following persons made significant contributions: Terry Boyle, Barry Jones, Tim Lundy, Tom Miller, Elizabeth Nash, Jim Neathery, Kim Poupart, Kari Stainback, Troy Stringfield, and Monty Waldron. It was my great pleasure to work with each of them and experience the image of Christ in them.

Others who shaped the Spiritual Formation program at Dallas Seminary from the early 1990s are John Contoveros, Pete Deison, Martin Hironaga, David Kanne, Dr. Bill Lawrence, Brad Smith, and David Ward. Special appreciation goes to Pete Deison and David Kanne for their early contribution to what eventually became *Life Story*, and to Dr. Bill Lawrence, who gave the team the freedom to "think outside the box" when he was the executive director of the Center for Christian Leadership. Dr. Andrew Seidel, the current acting executive director, has continued to provide needed support through the process of revising the series for use in churches and ministries. Kerri Gupta contributed much time and energy cleaning up the manuscript. Thanks to her for her editing work.

Dallas Theological Seminary provided the context and the resources necessary for this series. Many students have given valuable feedback in the development at various stages. The support of the seminary administration has been invaluable. This series could not have come into being without its support.

WILLIAM G. MILLER
Resource Development Coordinator
Center for Christian Leadership
Dallas Theological Seminary

A Model of Spiritual Transformation

What's the first thing that comes to mind when you think of spiritual growth? Some picture a solitary individual meditating or praying. While that concept accurately portrays one aspect of Christian spirituality, it doesn't tell the whole story.

Three Aspects of Transformation

The issue of spiritual transformation is not new in the Christian faith. It has been a primary issue, though perhaps given different labels, throughout church history. From the time the Spirit of God descended upon the believers in Jerusalem, God has been transforming the souls of individual believers in the context of local Christian communities.

Preaching has never been and never will be the only element needed for the transformation of Christians into Christ's image. Nor are small-group Bible studies, personal Bible study, Sunday school classes, or even one-on-one discipleship sufficient for growing Christians when they focus solely on communicating biblical information. Therefore, a movement has grown that emphasizes formation of the believer's inner and outer life and not just transformation of the intellect. Three broad approaches to spiritual transformation have developed.

Fellowship Model

One approach is to create fellowship opportunities. Churches develop structured settings for members to build relationships with others. They may launch small groups that meet in homes. They may convert their Sunday school classes into times of social engagement. These groups enable believers to be intimately involved in one another's lives. The fellowship model focuses on corporate prayer for one another, growth of interpersonal intimacy, and support for each other in times of need. This approach effectively connects believers within a church body.

Spiritual Disciplines Model

A second approach emphasizes disciplines such as meditation, prayer, fasting, and solitude. Such writers as Dallas Willard and Richard Foster have done excellent work on spiritual disciplines. This approach takes seriously the inner life and intimacy with God. However, when used in isolation, this approach can make people think spiritual transformation is a private matter. Even though the spiritual disciplines include communal elements (worship, service, and fellowship), some people treat the private exercises (silent retreats, journaling, meditating on Scripture, prayer, and fasting) as primary. That's a mistake.

Counseling Model

The third approach relies heavily on personal introspection. Christian counseling emphasizes areas of surrounding sin or personal character flaws that cause interpersonal problems or destructive behavior. Counseling seeks to understand the roots of such problems by looking at one's heritage and temperament. Usually in one-on-one interaction, the counselor probes for the root issues hidden beneath the surface problem. Discovering these deeper issues can shed light on a person's consistent failure to make wise choices. This approach focuses on identifying and dealing with those internal obstacles that prevent spiritual growth. Dealing with the issues is a key component in spiritual transformation.

The TRANSFORMING LIFE Model — An Integrated Approach

The three approaches are all valuable, but when taken alone they each have weaknesses. The fellowship model can fail to guide believers toward growth. The spiritual disciplines model can neglect to emphasize authentic and intimate Christian community, which is necessary for growth. The counseling model can fail to value the role that spiritual disciplines can have in growth. It also risks focusing on deficiencies so much that the person never benefits from the resources of God's grace. It can focus too intently upon the person's sin and failure and not enough on God's enabling power toward growth in holiness.

Therefore, TRANSFORMING LIFE brings in elements from all three approaches. The series tries to balance the inward and outward elements of transformation. Its theme is:

> Experiencing divine power through relationships;
> Striving together toward maturity in Christ.

We believe a particular context is essential to the transformation process. That context is authentic community in which people come to trust each other. Though one-on-one relationships can be effective, we believe that multiple relationships are more effective. While one individual can spur another toward growth, that one individual has limited gifts and abilities. Also, though we value the spiritual disciplines, we see them as means toward the end of complete transformation of the believer's inner and outer life. Disciplines aren't ends in themselves. Finally, we think believers need to seek greater understanding of sin's dynamic in their lives. They need to see potential blind spots or obstacles to their spiritual well-being and learn to deal with the root issues beneath their areas of struggle.

Our working definition of the Christian's transformation is:

> The process by which God forms Christ's character in believers by the ministry of the Spirit, in the context of community, and in accordance with biblical standards. This process involves the transformation of the whole person in thoughts, behaviors, and styles of relating with God and others. It results in a life of service to others and witness for Christ.

While the transformation process is an end in itself, the ultimate end is Christ's glory. He is the One adored by those who experience His presence and are transformed by Him. They, in turn, seek to exalt Him in the world.

Because each person is unique, God's formative process is unique for each. And though the Spirit of God is the One who transforms souls, each individual has personal responsibility in the process. Many spiritual disciplines can contribute, yet God is primarily concerned with transforming the whole person, not just patterns of behavior. For this reason, no one method (be it a traditional spiritual discipline or another method) is the single critical component.

A well-rounded experience of activities is the greatest catalyst for growth. For example, providing for the needy helps us better understand and participate in Christ's love for the outcast, needy, lonely, and depressed. A small group offers the chance to encourage a struggling believer, learn from others how to apply God's Word personally, and comfort someone in his or her grief. A regular time for prayer can help us reflect upon God's intimate love, remember personal needs and the needs of others as they are brought before God, release anxieties to God, and express dependence upon God. Spiritual formation occurs neither exclusively in private nor exclusively in public. For the character of Christ to be developed most fully, believers need an inner, private intimacy with God; an active, working love for others; and a pursuit of Christlike integrity.

TRANSFORMING LIFE depends solely on peer leadership. Groups don't need to be led by trained ministers. Leaders are more like facilitators—they don't need to have all the answers because group members learn from each other. The leader's role is to create an environment that fosters growth and encouragement.

Still, all small-group ministries need consistent coaching for the lay leaders. The group leaders need ministers and pastors to train and encourage them. A small-group ministry will raise all sorts of issues for leaders to deal with as people become honest about their lives in a trusting community. A group leader may need guidance about how to respond to a group member who shares that he has been having an e-mail "affair" and has not told his wife. Another leader may feel discouraged when group members drop out. Still another may wonder how to deal with two group members who are consistently angry with each other. It's important to provide support to those who take the risk to develop such an authentic environment for growth.

The Four Themes of This Series

Instead of aiming for competency in a set of skills or techniques, this series helps people identify the areas that must be developed in a believer's life. In other words, while it's necessary for a believer to know the "how-tos" of the Christian life, it's not sufficient. Knowing how to do personal Bible study and being good at sharing Christ with others are praiseworthy skills. Developing these skills, however, is not the end goal but the means by which we live out who we are as new creatures in Christ. That's why this series addresses four critical components of the Christian life: identity, community, integrity, and ministry.

This series proposes that the Christian life involves:

> knowing your identity in Christ
> *so that*
> you can make yourself known to others in a Christian community
> *so that*
> you can pursue a lifetime of growth in the context of community
> *so that*
> you are best equipped to glorify Christ by serving others.

Identity

To understand our need for transformation, we must understand who we are currently, both as individuals and as members of the body of Christ. Who we are has undoubtedly been shaped by our past. Therefore, we explore various aspects of our identity, such as our heritage and temperament. What do these tell us about who we are and what we value? The interaction during this study bonds us and builds trust among us. Our goal is not to analyze, criticize, or control each other, but it is to grow and affirm what God is doing in and through one another.

In *Identity*, we ultimately want group members to see themselves in light of their identity in Christ. However, many of the values we actually live out stem from such influences as temperament, family background, and culture. Not all of those values are contrary to our new identity in Christ. For example, the value one person places on honesty, which he learned from his parents, is affirmed by his identity in Christ.

It can take a long time—more than a lifetime allows—for the Spirit of God to transform our values to line up with our new identity in Christ. We cooperate with the Spirit when we reflect on what our values are and how well they line up with our identity in Christ as described in Scripture.

One very significant characteristic of our identity in Christ is that we are part of the body of Christ. The Christian life cannot be lived in isolation.

Community

So, while talking about *my* place in Christ, I need to pay attention to *our* place in Christ as a community. Understanding our corporate identity in

Christ is crucial for a healthy community transformation process. The *Community* study helps a group not only understand how a Christian community develops but also experience a growing sense of community.

In order to experience intimate community in the biblical sense, we must learn to reveal ourselves to others. We need to honestly, freely, and thoughtfully tell our stories. Our modern culture makes it easy for people to live isolated and anonymous lives. Because we and others move frequently, we may feel it's not worth the effort to be vulnerable in short-lived relationships. However, we desperately need to keep intentionally investing in significant relationships.

Real involvement in others' lives requires more than what the term *fellowship* has too often come to mean. Real involvement includes holding certain values in common and practicing a lifestyle we believe is noble, while appreciating that this lifestyle doesn't make us perfect. Rather, this lifestyle is a commitment to let God continue to spiritually form us.

Community includes a group exercise, "Life Story," that has been tremendously effective in building community and enhancing self-understanding. "Life Story" walks a person through the process of putting together a personal, creative presentation of the most formative relationships and experiences of his or her life. As people share their stories with each other, a deep level of trust and commitment grows.

Integrity

By the time a group has experienced *Identity* and *Community* together, members have built significant intimacy and trust. Now they're ready to pursue a harder step. It's the heart of our approach to spiritual transformation. Many believers greatly underestimate the necessity of intimacy and trust for successful growth in Christian holiness. But we must be able to share honestly those areas in which we need transformation. We can deal with deep issues of growth only in a community in which we're deeply known by others. We need others who have our best interests at heart. They must also be people we trust to hold sensitive issues in genuine confidence.

Why does the pursuit of Christian holiness need to occur in community? There are at least two reasons. First, we need accountability in the areas of sin with which we struggle. When we confess our struggles to a group, we become accountable to all of the members to press on toward growth. Because the group is aware of our sin, we can't hide it in darkness, where it retains a hold on our life and can make crippling guilt a permanent fixture in our walk. If we're struggling, we have not one but several people to lean on. In addition, the corporate, or group, setting increases the likelihood of support from someone else who has struggled in the same way. In one-on-one accountability, one person may not be able to relate well to the other's struggles. He or she may have different areas of struggle.

The second benefit of corporate pursuit of holiness is that without the encouragement and stimulus of other Christians, we're often blind to the ways in which we need to grow. In the counsel of many who care for us, there can be greater wisdom. If some believers are blind to being hospitable, the hospitality of another believer can spur them on to develop that quality in their own lives. If some never think about how to speak encouraging words, the encouraging speech of another can become contagious.

Ministry

With *Identity*, *Community*, and *Integrity* as a foundation, believers are prepared to discern how God wants them to serve in the body of Christ. "Where can I serve?" is not an optional question; every believer should ask it. Nor is this a matter simply for individual reflection. Rather, we can best discern where and how to serve while in community with people who know our past, interests, struggles, and talents. The community can affirm what they see in us and may know of opportunities to serve that we're unaware of.

How many terrific musicians are sitting in pews every Sunday because they lack the confidence to volunteer? Those gifted people might merely need others who know them well to encourage them to serve. Maybe someone's life story revealed that while growing up she played in a band. Someone might ask, "What have you done with that interest lately?"

The Layout of *Community*

Each session has the following features:
- *Session Aims* states a goal for you as an individual and one for the group.
- *Preparation* tells what assignment(s) you need to complete ahead of

time in order to get the most out of the group. For this study, much of the preparation will involve completing "Life Story" exercises. The "Life Story" exercises can be found on pages 61-96.

- *Introduction* sets up the session's topic.
- *Content* provides material around which group discussions and exercises will focus. You should read the "Introduction" and "Content" sections before your group meeting so you'll be prepared to discuss them.
- *Conclusion* wraps up the session and sets the scene for the next one.
- *Assignment* lists "homework" to complete before the next group meeting.

In this way, each session includes all three aspects of transformation: personal introspection, spiritual disciplines, and the experience of God in relationships. Through all of these means, the Spirit of God will be at work in your life.

A Method for the Biblical Exercise

The biblical exercise in session 6 will guide you through a self-study of a passage that relates to encouragement, counsel, and forgiveness. You'll begin by making observations about the passage. Pay attention to the following categories:

Who?

Identify persons in the passage: the descriptions of persons, the relationships between persons, and the conditions of persons.

What?

Identify subjects in the passage: the issues or topics being addressed.

When?

Identify time in the passage: duration of time that passes and when the events occurred in relationship to one another.

Where?

Identify places in the passage: the descriptions of locations, the relationships of places to other places, and the relationships of persons to the places.

Why?

Identify purposes in the passage: the expressions of purpose by the author and/or the characters.

How?

Identify events in the passage: the descriptions of events unfolding, the relationships between events, and the order of events.

In *Living By the Book*, Dr. Howard Hendricks and William Hendricks identify six categories that aid the process of observation. They encourage readers to "look for things that are (1) emphasized, (2) repeated, (3) related, (4) alike, (5) unalike, or (6) true to life."[1]

After you make observations, you will interpret the passage. Interpretation involves determining what the main point of the passage is. Then you'll reflect on how the main point applies to your life. Be sure to ask for God's guidance in your reflection. After all, the purpose of Scripture is for God to speak to us and, as a result, for our lives to be transformed.

God's Authorship

Creating a community isn't easy, but it's worth it. To meet with a group, get to know the individuals, and acquire cognitive facts about them definitely helps you build community, but these components on their own don't guarantee real community.

It's also helpful to know certain principles that contribute to deep, rich community. This study will address some of those principles, but even knowing them isn't enough. Something more is necessary, but it's hard to obtain because it can't be measured or quantified. This essential element is trust.

So the goal of this study is *for group members to pursue new depths of trust with each other out of a common commitment to discovering God's authorship in their own lives.* Instead of just studying the concept of biblical community, your group will work through a tool called "Life Story" to build trust and establish community. As you work through "Life Story," you will first examine your life and then present it to others as stories authored by God.

But first, what does it mean to say that God is the Author of your life?

Session Aims

Individual Aim: To recognize that each person's life is a story authored by God.

Group Aim: To discuss God's authorship of people's lives and the responsibility individuals have for their own actions and choices.

Preparation

Read *Session 1: God's Authorship.*

Read *Life Story: Introduction* beginning on page 61.

Read *Life Story: Step A* beginning on page 63.

Introduction

It's been said that the most powerful words are "Once upon a time." The listener immediately perks up and wants to hear what will follow. Whether fictional or historical, a well-told story has dramatic impact. Some of our most vivid memories of Scripture are stories: David and Goliath, Daniel and the lions' den, Jesus walking on the water. Jesus understood the power of stories and used parables as one of His main methods of teaching. He used stories to communicate with His followers in a meaningful and life-changing way.

Stories can communicate meaning far more powerfully than most people realize. When people begin telling stories from their own life experience, you can sense the emotion in their voice. Often you can observe more excitement or intensity in their words when they tell personal stories. That's why telling stories about experiences that have most influenced and shaped your life is a deeply personal exercise. Taken together, those most significant stories are "your story." Do you realize that you have a story? Even more important, do you know that your story reflects the authorship of God?

Content

In order to genuinely be a part of a community, you must be able to tell your story. People must be exposed to your happenings and your heart. But in a Christian community, telling personal stories will always include, as a crucial component, your experience of God's providence, salvation, and sanctification. To tell stories in this manner, you need to learn to observe what God has been doing in your life. The result will be an act of worship as you express and respond to expressions of God's goodness and love.

This study's fundamental exercise, "Life Story," answers the question "How has God authored my story up to this point in my life?" This question immediately raises more questions:
- How does God's sovereignty fit with the freewill decisions that have shaped my past?
- What does God's authorship really mean?
- Has God written a screenplay through which I must simply walk with little or no control over the outcome? Or am I a player on a stage with no script at all?

Though at times you might like to subscribe to one of the views suggested in the last question, neither scenario is accurate. Humans are inherently limited in their ability to understand how divine sovereignty and human responsibility (also known as predestination versus free will) fit together. So as you and your group review the events in your lives and speak of God authoring your stories, try to avoid blaming God for any painful or sinful actions of others or yourselves. On the other hand, don't ignore God's control of the events.

Consider the life of Joseph. He was able to rightly reconcile his brothers' sinful actions—which really and negatively affected his life—with God's control over his life. In Genesis 45:4-5 he said, "I am your brother Joseph, the one you sold into Egypt! And now, do not be distressed and do not be angry with yourselves for selling me here, because it was to save lives that God sent me ahead of you." And in Genesis 50:19-20 he said, "Don't be afraid. Am I in the place of God? You intended to harm me, but God intended it for good to accomplish what is now being done, the saving of many lives."

Regarding Joseph and his statements, theologian D. A. Carson comments,

> He (Joseph) did not picture the event as wicked human machination into which God intervened to bring forth good. Nor did he imagine God's intention had been to send him down there with a fine escort and a modern chariot but that unfortunately the brothers had mucked up the plan and so poor Joseph had to go down there as a slave. Rather, in one and the same event, God was operating and His intentions were good, and the brothers' intentions were evil.[1]

Scripture doesn't try to explain how these conflicting intentions are compatible; it merely states that they are.

Perhaps no event displays this conundrum more than the death of Christ. Peter prayed this regarding the death of Christ: "Indeed Herod and Pontius Pilate met together with the Gentiles and the people of Israel in this city to conspire against your holy servant Jesus, whom you anointed. They did what your power and will had decided beforehand should happen" (Acts 4:27-28). In the same action, Herod, Pilate, the Romans, and the Jews committed the greatest miscarriage of justice in the history of the world.

Yet this atrocious act fit with God's plan. Again, Carson's insight is helpful in highlighting the significance of this concept in our doctrine:

> A moment's reflection discloses that any other account of what happened would destroy Christianity. If the crucifixion of Jesus Christ is pictured solely in terms of the conspiracy of the local political authorities at the time, and not in terms of God's plan (except perhaps that He decided at the last moment to use the death in a way He Himself had not foreseen), then this means the Cross was an accident of history. If it were an accident cleverly manipulated by God in His own interests, but not part of the divine plan, then the entire pattern of antecedent predictive revelation would be destroyed (including the Day of Atonement, the Passover lamb, the sacrificial system, and so forth). On the other hand if a person stresses God's sovereignty in Jesus' death, exulting that all the participants "did what your power and will had decided beforehand should happen" (4:28), while forgetting that it was a wicked conspiracy, then Herod, Pilate, Judas Iscariot, and the rest are exonerated of evil. If God's sovereignty means that everyone under it is immune from charges of transgression, then there is no sin for which atonement is necessary. So why the Cross? Either way, the Cross is destroyed.[2]

As you begin to explore your story in detail, you will face the same issue of human responsibility and God's sovereignty. Inevitably, events in your life will seem inconsistent with God's authorship. Sinful choices, others' cruelty, rejection, disappointment, sickness, and even death mark everyone's life. Exploring your life can turn into an exercise of bitterness if you blame God for such events and actions. You can also go astray or feel disillusioned if you label "good" those things that God would never call "good." By faith, you must recognize that all of the events in your life are compatible with God's sovereignty. Some of those events require faith that God is in control. The compatibility between your free will and God's sovereignty will not always answer your questions. Instead, the mysterious compatibility of the two can cause you to recognize and accept both that God is in control over the world and that humans still exercise their own responsibility.

To reap the benefits of your story, you must believe in God's power in all of life. As Paul explained to the Athenians, "The God who made the world

and everything in it . . . he himself gives all men life and breath and everything else. . . . 'For in him we live and move and have our being'" (Acts
17:24-25,28).

Conclusion

You can submit intellectually to the compatibility between human responsibility and God's sovereignty, but that doesn't always ease the emotions of
grappling with the hard parts of your story. As you begin to think and pray
through your life, ask God to use this exercise to strengthen your faith in
Him as the Author of your story.

Assignment

Complete *Life Story: Step A* beginning on page 63.

Read *Session 2: Experiences and Relationships.*

Read *Life Story: Step B* beginning on page 73.

Experiences and Relationships

In session 1, you saw that God's sovereignty and human responsibility are compatible. With that principle in mind, you'll now consider how specific experiences and relationships have affected your life. Though you may not always be aware of it, your personal history has played a central part in shaping your life. You'll now begin looking back on your personal history.

Session Aims

Individual Aim: To begin to think about the effects of past experiences and relationships.

Group Aim: To recognize the value of recalling past experiences and relationships and to understand how "Life Story" facilitates this process.

Preparation

Complete *Life Story: Step A* beginning on page 63.

Read *Session 2: Experiences and Relationships.*

Read *Life Story: Step B* beginning on page 73.

Introduction

Christians have different opinions about how believers should think about their past. One extreme view focuses entirely on the past as the key to understanding one's present life situation. This view largely ignores the way God has worked in the past to form each believer as His unique child. Those who hold this view think past experience entirely determines a person's behavior patterns; God seems to be absent from the picture.

The opposite extreme sees a person's past, particularly his or her preconversion past, as entirely irrelevant to the present. Those in this camp rightly recognize that they have become new creatures in Christ. However, based on that concept, they conclude that no past experiences have any influence on their new life. They try to leave all aspects of their identity behind and build a new identity from a blank slate. This view also ignores any possibility that God was at work in people's lives before their salvation.

Scripture passages could be found to support either extreme, but this study seeks to avoid both extremes. So instead of defending either side, you will take a long look into your past to examine God's handiwork.

Content

Consider the apostle Paul's view of his past experiences and relationships. On the surface, it might seem Paul viewed all of his preconversion life as irrelevant. This view might be drawn from Philippians 3, in which Paul writes about certain aspects of his preconversion life and concludes,

> But whatever was to my profit I now consider loss for the sake of Christ. What is more, I consider everything a loss compared to the surpassing greatness of knowing Christ Jesus my Lord, for whose sake I have lost all things. I consider them rubbish, that I may gain Christ. (verses 7-8)

Did Paul hold that examining his past was irrelevant? Look at how he used his past experiences and relationships in other passages.

In his letter to the Galatians, Paul recounted at length his persecution of the church, his zeal in Judaism, his time in Arabia, his preaching in Syria and Cilicia, and his confrontation of Peter (see Galatians 1:11–2:21). His efforts to seek death sentences for Christ's followers took place before his conversion, yet he thought this episode was relevant enough to discuss not only with the Galatians but also many years later with his protégé Timothy (see 1 Timothy 1:12-13). To the Corinthians he described beatings, stonings, shipwrecks, and other physical and emotional hardships endured for the gospel (see 2 Corinthians 11:21-33). When addressing a crowd in Jerusalem, he told his story, emphasizing his Jewish ethnicity, birth in Tarsus, training under a famous rabbi, persecution of the church, and details of his conversion (see Acts 22:1-21).

Paul used his life story for several purposes: to teach, evangelize, and even defend himself. Aspects of his past had ongoing effects throughout his life. Pragmatically, he used his Roman citizenship to avoid an unlawful beating (see Acts 22:25-29). Spiritually, his past contributed to his awe of God's grace in forgiving his preconversion crimes (see 1 Timothy 1:15-16; Ephesians 3:8).

Conclusion

Paul's constructive use of his past shows that he didn't view examination of his past as a futile effort. He used his past to learn about himself and God. In light of this evidence, how should Philippians 3 be interpreted? Paul's point was that his past experiences and relationships contributed nothing *to gaining righteousness*. However, the passage doesn't say his past experiences and relationships held no value for his present life. In fact, his use of the past in Philippians 3 demonstrates that he had carefully considered his past:

> *If anyone else thinks he has reasons to put confidence in the flesh, I have more: circumcised on the eighth day, of the people of Israel, of the tribe of Benjamin, a Hebrew of Hebrews; in regard to the law, a Pharisee; as for zeal, persecuting the church; as for legalistic righteousness, faultless. (verses 4-6)*

He counted all of this as useless for earning God's approval, but he understood how much this past history had shaped him for God's service. And above all, his past moved him to worship the God who forgives.

Assignment

Complete *Life Story: Step B* beginning on page 73.

Read *Session 3: Formative Elements and Themes.*

Read *Life Story: Steps C, D, E,* and *F* beginning on page 77.

Formative Elements and Themes

In session 2 you saw how past experiences and relationships can affect a Christian's current life. In "Life Story: Step B," you identified and recorded the significant experiences and relationships of your past. You will now seek to interpret the data you recorded.

This interpretive process begins as you identify your *most formative* experiences and relationships. You'll then examine the concept of *theme*. To contribute to an authentic community, you need to tell your story not just as a series of facts but also as an account full of meaning and God's purposes.

Session Aims

Individual Aim: To identify formative experiences and relationships and to identify major themes in your life story.

Group Aim: To discuss how to discern the most formative experiences and relationships in a story and determine the theme.

Preparation

Complete *Life Story: Step B* beginning on page 73.

Read *Session 3: Formative Elements and Themes*.

Read *Life Story: Steps C, D, E,* and *F* beginning on page 77.

Introduction

David didn't suddenly achieve prowess with a slingshot on the day when he met and killed Goliath (see 1 Samuel 17). God had allowed David years of experience in sheep pastures, where he learned skills he could use for God's purposes. Likewise, David was probably as incredulous as his father was when Samuel anointed David king of Israel (see 1 Samuel 16). But God had long been at work behind the scenes in his young life. Years later, David reviewed elements of his life story in his psalms. David saw God's hand at work throughout his life, even in the darkest moments, and he used his own story as an act of worship.

This connection between worship and "Life Story" is crucial. You're going to organize the formative elements of your life into a story that recognizes God as the key figure, the One who brought you to this point. Your story will be a hymn of praise. Your group's hymns will draw your group together into community in an extraordinary way.

Content

You can view your life story at two levels. First, you can see the fine detail of times when God seemed particularly and intimately involved. Second, you can step back and recognize God's overarching plan, the broad strokes of His work in your life. Those broad strokes involve themes and trends.

God's intimate involvement usually appears in your formative experiences and relationships. Work with these first because they are the building blocks of larger themes.

Formative experiences and relationships are those that have had lasting effects — they have molded and shaped you. Last week you compiled an extensive list of experiences and relationships. Now you'll distinguish which of those events and people have had the most significant effects on you.

> *formative:* 1. giving form or shape; forming; shaping; fashioning; molding 2. pertaining to formation or development[1]

Many of your most formative experiences and relationships may be ones you least enjoy thinking about (stressful times, relationships with conflict, or tragic losses). Others may be your most enjoyable and exciting past relationships and experiences. And you shouldn't overlook those formative experiences and relationships that developed through mundane circumstances. The key issue is the *lasting effect* these people and events have had on you.

What makes an experience or relationship formative? It has one or more of the following traits:

- You can see a significant meaning or purpose in it—it seems to have happened "for a reason."
- You know it has shaped who you've become even if you can't see why God allowed it to happen. By faith you trust that God is using this experience constructively in your life or other people's lives, even though it has been painful and you don't yet see the fruit.
- It stands out to you as a pillar of God's faithfulness in your life.

For further explanation of these three traits, see their descriptions in "Life Story: Step C" beginning on page 77.

> *meaning:* 1. that which is intended to be, or actually is, expressed or indicated; signification; import 2. the end, purpose, or significance of something[2]

> *purpose:* 1. the reason for which something exists or is done, made, used, etc. 2. an intended or desired result; end; aim; goal[3]

Once you've identified the specific experiences and relationships that have shaped you, you can step back and look for themes and trends that arise from the whole picture.

> *theme:* In literature, the central or dominating idea, the "message," implicit in a work. The theme of a work is seldom stated directly. It is an abstract concept indirectly expressed through recurrent images, actions, characters, and symbols, and must be inferred by the reader or spectator. Theme differs from subject (the topic or thing described in a work) in that theme is a comment, observation, or insight about the subject. For example, the subject of a poem may be a flower; its theme, a comment on the fleeting nature of existence.[4]

For example, success might be a thread running through your story. Your mother talked about the importance of financial success. You experienced your father's long hours at the office when you were growing up and the financial rewards that eventually came to your family. You had to work hard to attain good enough grades at school, but the effort seems to be linked to the career you were able to launch. Those are the facts of your story. But the *meaning* you attached to your father's absence from home during the evenings was not "The pursuit of financial gain weakens family bonds." Rather, through your mother's influence, you attached the meaning "Success comes through perseverance." You attached the same meaning to your school experience and later to your career experience. Thus, as you look at the broad sweep of your story, you can see this idea emerging as a consistent theme: "Success comes through perseverance."

Other examples of themes include: "Contentment is a product of contemplation," "Discernment attained through counsel can conquer confusion," and "Deception will reap personal destruction." A theme evaluates *how an element* (such as success, contentment, discernment, deception, or education) *affects that person's relationships, perceptions, and decisions.*

Theme is the consistent pattern of how an issue is addressed as a story develops. As you step back to consider how events and relationships in your life connect to provide meaning, one or more themes likely will emerge.

Conclusion

Now that you have addressed some basic issues for discerning the most formative elements of your story, you are equipped to finish the preparation of your "Life Story" presentation. We hope this discussion of what types of content you ought to address will help you share the most meaningful parts of your story with your community.

The upcoming sessions will begin to discuss other qualities that contribute to an authentic Christian community. These principles will be fundamental building blocks for your group to experience a healthy community.

Assignment

Complete *Life Story: Step* C beginning on page 77.

Read *Session 4: The Art of Speech*.

Read *Life Story: Step* G beginning on page 95.

The Art of Speech

There is an art to speaking well. You can notice this every day as you listen to people gifted in speech on the radio or television. However, the ability to speak well in an intimate setting is very different from what is needed in a large public setting. In order to serve and love others in an intimate, community setting, you need to be able to speak well and listen well. (You'll address listening later.)

Speaking well in a community includes telling personal stories. Your story is more than what you can write on paper. For your story to achieve its ultimate purpose, you must share it with others in an effective and genuine fashion. Though you may have been greatly blessed by the process of assembling your life story, the true impact comes from sharing it with others. Sharing stories with one another, as you will experience, is a powerful instrument for building community.

Session Aims

Individual Aim: To learn how to share your life through personal stories in an inviting and influential manner.

Group Aim: To consider how the way you tell your stories affects the process of building community.

Preparation

Complete *Life Story: Step* C beginning on page 77.

Read *Session 4: The Art of Speech*.

Read *Life Story: Step* G beginning on page 95.

Introduction

Thinking about your life as a story broken up into chapters and themes is a different way of looking at personal history than you may be used to. People often communicate stories as a string of events. Unfortunately, this approach gives no emphasis or highlighting. For instance, "I was fifteen when I got saved, and then I worked that summer as a lifeguard, and then I went to college, and then I was not walking with God, and then I . . ." Ideally, by diligently examining your life and working through its chapters and themes, you will avoid this type of communication.

When you share a personal story with others, even a simple story about how your day has gone, you don't need a charismatic personality. The story should invite others into your life. It should also influence them as it acknowledges God, as it tells your story as one character within His story. Group members may learn, face challenges, find encouragement, or respond with thanksgiving and worship as a result of hearing your story. If nothing else, they should see God's grace and faithfulness.

Content

It's important to tell an inviting and influential story. You won't fully achieve the purpose of sharing your story if you can't effectively communicate it to the group. But storytelling scares some people. Maybe you hate being the center of attention or fear you'll look foolish. To alleviate any fears, let's look at several key elements of communication that are particularly relevant to telling stories.

Engagement

Communicating with others at the level of intimacy involved in sharing personal stories requires the engagement of both the speaker and the listeners. In his book *Creating Understanding*, Donald Smith describes this level of communication:

> It may be called reciprocity, dialogue, or co-response, but whatever the name, the basis of effective communication is mutual involvement of sender and receiver. It must be the special concern of

the initiator of communication to ensure the involvement of the participants.[1]

Elsewhere, Smith states, "Communication is a relationship. We do not get involved in order to communicate. We communicate by being involved. Involvement is the foundation of all communication."[2] When sharing our stories, we reach a level of involvement in one another's lives that bonds us together.

However, anytime we invite people into our lives and hope to communicate who we truly are, we feel a level of insecurity. We might fear rejection: "If I tell them that I ran away from home in high school after getting my girlfriend pregnant, they will never look at me the same way. Maybe they'll withdraw from me." This kind of insecurity can make us hold back the most significant aspects of our stories. In fact, there may be times you are just not ready to tell certain chapters from your story. However, if you develop a pattern of holding back your most life-changing chapters, you will limit intimacy. People won't see any way to engage with you if you don't engage with them in this way. Insecurities must be overcome.

Another aspect of engagement is to involve yourself in what you are saying. Communicate your story with the emotion that is inherent in the content. It's your life, so it's significant to you. Avoid thinking it's irrelevant to others. People want to hear you tell it, so tell it with passion. When you do so, you will naturally engage with others.

It is important to give a warning at this point against "dumping" your stories on people without the appropriate context of relationship. Though we want to encourage you to share your stories, we don't want to encourage you to go through life telling every person you run into your most personal stories. That can make others feel awkward and wonder why someone they don't feel they know well or trust is telling them such personal things. Trust is built between people over time as they reveal more and more personal things and feel that the other people increasingly honor what they share.

Cohesion

In order to use all of the information you cataloged in "Life Story" to its greatest potential, you need to bring the many details together into concise units of meaning. Haddon Robinson notes,

The ability to abstract and synthesize, that is, to think in ideas, develops with maturity. Small children think in particulars. A child praying at breakfast thanks God for the milk, cereal, orange juice, eggs, bread, butter, and jelly, but an adult combines all these separate items into the single word *food*. An idea, therefore, may be considered a distillation of life. It abstracts out of the particulars of life what they have in common and relates them to each other. Through ideas we make sense out of the parts of our experience.[3]

The "Life Story" tool has guided you in this process of turning details into meaningful concepts. As the chapters of your life take form and themes emerge, your work is transformed into a story. When telling a story, you're communicating not just factual information but also a meaningful message about your understanding of yourself, the world, others, and God. Use your presentation as an opportunity to practice and develop your ability to tell stories in a more meaningful way.

As with engagement, insecurities can prevent you from effectively communicating a cohesive story. As you prepare to share a concise account of twenty, thirty, forty, or more years of life, you may fear that your listeners won't fully understand you. This insecurity may tempt you to exceed an appropriate amount of time and inundate your listeners with every detail of your story. But all these details often muddle a story rather than clarify it. The goal of synthesis is to bring meaning, and the goal of the presentation is to create understanding. Bringing out every detail won't help you reach these goals; instead, it will hinder you. The key to communicating a cohesive story is to note the significant points and develop them in relation to the themes of your life.

Delivery and Style

Friedrich Nietzsche said, "He who knows himself to be profound endeavors to be clear; he who would like to appear profound to the crowd endeavors to be obscure."[4] Don't try to appear more profound or complex than you are. Your life is an important part in God's larger story; it doesn't need to be dressed up. You don't need to belittle or augment your story.

You will be most effective when your delivery and style are natural. If you are a low-key person, don't try to be gregarious. If you are an upbeat person, don't try to be somber. Seek to develop a style of communicating that is consistent with your personality. There are laid-back people who are just as compelling to listen to when they tell personal stories as life-of-the-party people.

However, insecurities can once again prevent success in this area. Insecurities can affect delivery and style in ways that impede true communication. At one extreme are those people who are so self-conscious of how they come across that they don't communicate naturally. Focus on communicating effectively and creating understanding rather than on protecting your image. The other extreme of insecurity surfaces in those people who put on a major production of their stories. They hide behind storytelling performances that might dazzle a group, but they would be far more effective in connecting with the group if they engaged and were willing to be themselves. Donald Smith adds,

> Sending and receiving messages can be coldly impersonal, a separate thing from real communication. Effective communication that leads to deep comprehension and response occurs only through involvement in each other's life and interests. Without involvement, the most skilled use of media and techniques may be only an imitation of communication.[5]

Setting

The setting in which you communicate will affect your delivery, cohesion, and engagement. You may engage differently in a private setting (such as a home) than you would in a public setting (such as a restaurant or office). If you're driving while telling a story, you can't have optimal eye contact.

Also, time constraints affect the degree of cohesion you can develop. You may not have time to tell all the essential details of the story.

Finally, the setting may affect your style and delivery. For example, the way you would tell your husband you're pregnant would depend on your surroundings. In an upscale restaurant with a quiet atmosphere, you would likely tone down your boisterous demeanor when communicating your excitement. But if sharing the news at home, you might be louder and more expressive.

Envision yourself waiting with a friend and coworker for a meeting in the foyer outside a conference room. The meeting is scheduled to start in five minutes, and you won't have any time to talk with your friend afterward. You want to tell this person that your father was just diagnosed with cancer and that you have been struggling with the news. In light of the circumstances, you have to determine the most private setting available, so you motion for your friend to move to the corner of the room with you. Given the parameters, you may not be able to share all the memories of your dad that you've been thinking about. However, you will be able to share the heart of the matter: You're afraid your father might not live much longer. In addition, you want to share that you are really struggling to hold yourself together. You will obviously need to communicate all this with the emotion appropriate to the circumstances. At some other time, you'll need to reveal these heartaches in more detail with those to whom you are closest and in a very private and unhurried setting.

This example involves engagement, cohesion, delivery, style, and setting. It demonstrates how these four components can, when understood and developed, contribute to deep, fulfilling relationships. Developing these skills will help you become a better member of a community.

Conclusion

As you prepare to present your life story with your group, remember that you have a predetermined amount of time to convey your story. Strive to honor the time constraints. You are communicating to a small community that is developing trust. The group members are friends, not foes, who should provide a setting of encouragement. Invite them into your life and influence them through your story.

Assignment

Complete *Life Story: Step D* beginning on page 81.

Read *Session 5: Listening.*

Listening

Communication requires both a sender and a receiver of information. In the last session, you focused on your responsibilities as the sender. Now let's look at the receiver's responsibilities. Listening well is vital for authentic Christian community. It will determine how vulnerably people will communicate. It will affect how much you learn about others and about God's work in them. Learning how to listen well to others' stories is imperative.

Session Aims

Individual Aim: To learn how to become a better listener.

Group Aim: To discuss the necessity of good listening in order to achieve understanding and mutual encouragement.

Preparation

Complete *Life Story: Step D* beginning on page 81.

Read *Session 5: Listening*.

Introduction

> *Do nothing out of selfish ambition or vain conceit, but in humility consider others better than yourselves. Each of you should look not only to your own interests, but also to the interests of others. (Philippians 2:3-4)*

In order to live by these verses, you must listen to others well. After all, how can you know the interests of others without listening carefully to them?

Content

There are two broad categories of communication: verbal and nonverbal. Nonverbal forms include silence, sounds (like "hmmm," "ahh!" and tapping a foot), body motions, facial expressions, posture, touch, and even smell. You may be far less conscious of your nonverbal forms of communication than of your words.

However, receivers of communication tend to trust the nonverbal forms more than verbal ones. In particular, people will trust your body language more than your words. For instance, if you say you're at peace but your body language (facial expression, trembling hands) says you're anxious, then people will distrust your words.

You may not realize how many nonverbal signal systems are at work when you communicate. The heart of your message is carried in these nonverbal signals, many of which you are using unconsciously. And as a listener, you are affected by these signals whether you know it or not. How many times have you left a conversation and said to yourself, *I heard what he was saying, but I sure sensed something strange about it?* You picked up on the nonverbal signals, but you just didn't know what to do with them.

Keep nonverbal communication in mind as you prepare to listen to others' "Life Story" presentations. Your aim shouldn't be merely to take in the data the speaker is presenting. Your ultimate concern should be to love others when you listen. One part of loving the speaker is to take in his or her story's significance and respond to it in a loving way.

Even as you silently listen, you are communicating nonverbally to the presenter. For example, if a friend begins telling you something personal and you stare off into the sky, you are saying, "I'm not interested." To love him or her, you need to focus on receiving the information accurately *and* on sending nonverbal messages of commitment and trust.

Finally, a crucial part of responding in love is to keep others' stories confidential. When group members share their life stories, it must be clear to all the members that the stories are confidential. This is especially critical in a church or ministry setting in which many people in the larger community know each other. If a group member repeats parts of another group member's story, all the trust that may have been previously built collapses. Rebuilding that same level of trust will be extremely difficult, if not impossible.

Confidentiality is equally necessary when others share personal stories in the broader context of life. If you stop to think before you speak, you normally know whether a story you heard from one person should not be shared with others. A good rule of thumb is to ask yourself, *Would I tell this story about her if she were here?* A failure to maintain confidentiality in your interpersonal relationships is like a cancer in a local church body or ministry. Such behavior will also hinder your witness with the nonbelieving world that watches you.

Conclusion

Look at your "Life Story" worksheets and note the sections for life divisions, titles, experiences and relationships, what you learn about God and self, and themes. Not only do you need to be attentive to these things in your own life so you can present your story, but you also need to attentively listen to these aspects of others' stories. Truly understanding a person presenting his or her life story is a great challenge. It's essential to listen well with the intent of entering into the person's life for mutual understanding and encouragement.

Assignment

Complete *Life Story: Steps E* and *F* beginning on page 83.

Complete the *Biblical Exercise: Ephesians 4* beginning on page 43.

Read *Session 6: Encouragement, Counsel, and Forgiveness*.

Encouragement, Counsel, and Forgiveness

Session 5 focused on the important role listening plays in creating understanding and building trust. However, good listening is not the end of responding lovingly to those who tell their stories. Three more traits of loving response are encouragement, counsel, and forgiveness. In this session, you will discuss how these qualities contribute to building community.

Session Aims

Individual Aim: To learn how to offer encouragement and counsel and how to experience forgiveness.

Group Aim: To understand the significance of encouragement, counsel, and forgiveness in the process of building community.

Preparation

Complete *Life Story: Steps E* and *F* beginning on page 83.

Complete *Biblical Exercise: Ephesians 4*.

Read *Session 6: Encouragement, Counsel, and Forgiveness*.

Biblical Exercise: Ephesians 4

Read Ephesians 4:17-32. Also, review "A Method for the Biblical Exercise" beginning on page 17.

Observation — **"What Do I See?"**

1. Who are the persons (including God) in the passage? What is the condition of those persons?

2. What subjects did Paul discuss in the passage? What did he assert?

3. Note the sequence in which Paul made these assertions. (You might number them in order.)

4. What did Paul emphasize? Are there repeated ideas and themes? How are the various parts related?

5. Why did Paul write this passage? (Did he say anything about ways he expected the reader to change after reading it?)

Interpretation Phase 1—**"What Did It Mean Then?"**

1. Coming to Terms—Are there any words in the passage that you don't understand? Write down anything you found confusing about the passage.

2. Finding Where It Fits—What clues does the Bible give about the meaning of this passage?

- Immediate Context (the passage being studied)

- Remote Context (passages that come before and after the one being studied)

3. Getting into Their Sandals—An Exercise in Imagination

- What are the main points of this passage? Summarize or write an outline of it.

- What do you think the recipients of the letter were supposed to take from this passage? How did God, inspiring Paul to write Ephesians, want this passage to impact the Ephesian believers?

Interpretation Phase 2—**"What Does It Mean Now?"**

1. What is the timeless truth in the passage? In one or two sentences, write down what you learned about God from Ephesians 4.

2. How does that truth work today?

Application—**"What Can I Do to Make This Truth Real?"**

1. What can I do to make this truth real for myself?

2. For my family?

3. For my friends?

4. For the people who live near me?

5. For the rest of the world?

Introduction

As you explore encouragement, counsel, and forgiveness, it's worth remembering the purpose of the study: for group members to pursue new depths of trust with each other out of a common commitment to discovering God's authorship in their lives.

Encouragement, counsel, and forgiveness are all present or implied in the description in Hebrews 10:24-25 of loving Christian community:

> And let us consider how we may spur one another on toward love and good deeds. Let us not give up meeting together, as some are in the habit of doing, but let us encourage one another—and all the more as you see the Day approaching.

Though forgiveness is not explicitly mentioned, one can hardly imagine a group of diverse believers meeting together consistently without ever needing to forgive one another. In Ephesians 4:17-32, which you studied, Paul wrote explicitly about forgiveness in an encouraging and edifying community:

> Be kind and compassionate to one another, forgiving each other, just as in Christ God forgave you. (Ephesians 4:32)

Content

Most of us are well aware of our responsibility to encourage one another. The Bible tells us that what we say to others can bring great blessing and healing. "A man finds joy in giving an apt reply—and how good is a timely word!" (Proverbs 15:23). "A word aptly spoken is like apples of gold in settings of silver" (Proverbs 25:11).

So why do we often struggle to give encouraging words? James reminds us that no one can tame the tongue, which is a fire that can blaze out of control (see James 3:1-8). Controlling our words is difficult. We know that "the tongue has the power of life and death, and those who love it will eat its fruit" (Proverbs 18:21). But how do we bring forth that life-giving power? Counselors Larry Crabb and Dan Allender suggest that we must overcome the obstacle of "surface community." They write,

> What prevents our words from having power? How do we bridge the distance between us and others so that what we say bears weight? Offering an answer requires that we first understand the problem of surface community, a kind of relational structure that prevents words from realizing their potential to encourage.[1]

No matter how hard we may try to say the "correct" words, certain forces work for or against us, going beyond the words we speak. The great force we want working for us is the Holy Spirit through authentic community. Our words lose power, are easily misunderstood, or fall on deaf ears when spoken in a superficial or surface community.

A "surface community" may be divided by walls of fear, insecurity, self-protection, lack of trust, and individualism, but the answer to breaking down those walls is not unrestrained sharing. Crabb and Allender note that "sharing feelings without a prior and overriding commitment to the welfare of the other leads to disunity, not unity."[2] Unleashing our feelings is not always the path to authentic community and others' encouragement. This is true for both the one telling a story and the one responding. We should share personal stories authentically and vulnerably with those we have come to trust. Sharing in this way with a stranger is unwise. Likewise, it's often unwise to offer counsel to someone with whom you have no credibility. Constructive counsel should be shared within a relationship of trust.

Commitment to others is the crucial element. As we demonstrate commitment, trust builds. Paul describes the real meaning of commitment like this:

> *Do not let any unwholesome talk come out of your mouths, but only what is helpful for building others up according to their needs, that it may benefit those who listen. (Ephesians 4:29)*

Choosing to share the right words at the right time in response to another's deeply personal story can be a powerful source of encouragement. But how do we determine the right words and the right time? Crabb and Allender offer three important principles to keep in mind. The first of these principles states, "The essence of encouragement is exposure without rejection":

> It is true that Christians are fully accepted by God because of Jesus' shed blood. For us, there is now no condemnation. But somehow we fail to grasp that God's acceptance makes anyone else's rejection no more devastating than a misplaced dollar would be to a millionaire. We foolishly believe that other people's acceptance represents a legitimate measure of our value. We fear the rejection of people and therefore hide from them.[3]

We can't hide ourselves from one another out of fear of rejection if we want our shared stories to encourage us. Sharing stories involves sharing the joys and sorrows, the successes and failures, the aspirations and disappointments of life. This kind of sharing requires vulnerability. Meeting such vulnerability with acceptance produces encouragement.

Crabb and Allender's second principle of encouragement states, "Understanding is sometimes better than advice":

> Lost people need direction. Blind people need enlightening. Stubborn people need prodding. Clear instruction on how to handle life's problems is obviously necessary. But people are not only lost, blind, and stubborn; they are also scared. And scared people need patient, accepting understanding. Christians must grasp the apparently elusive truth that advice without understanding is not helpful. It is in fact a form of rejection. Quick advice communicates disrespect and disinterest. The words spoken may be "I think you

should . . . " The words heard may be "Your problem is simple. But you're too stupid to figure out a solution. So I'll tell you what to do."[4]

Rather than counsel, people initially need someone who understands. Counsel may be helpful and needed, but only after compassion and acceptance.

Crabb and Allender's third principle is, "The more precise the understanding, the more encouraging the words." This principle involves more than just understanding what people say. Crabb and Allender suggest that it involves understanding the deep needs we all share for "relationship and meaning," "love and purpose," or "security and significance":

> The essential fear that is locked deep in the core of fallen people is the fear of insecurity (rejection) and insignificance (loss of value). If encouragers clearly understand that these two deep longings lie beneath people's layers of self-sufficiency, their words may reflect a greater understanding of people's fear. . . . Encouragers will be sensitive to ways in which they can pick up on the basic needs and say something that can bring hope to a person who otherwise might despair of ever experiencing the security and significance available in Christ. A precise understanding of people's needs can assist the encourager to be more encouraging.[5]

Our ability to listen well to both the verbal and nonverbal forms of communication determines the level at which we can encourage and give counsel to others. For instance, if we hear well enough to respond with, "Boy, that sounds tough," we are either not listening well or not willing to engage at a personal level. In contrast, to respond to an intimate story with, "How has your dad's abuse of you as a kid affected your ability to love your kids?" communicates profound encouragement and begins to open the possibility for offering counsel. The person not only will feel heard but also that he or she is being pursued and appreciated, so he or she will be more likely to ask for and receive counsel.

When we respond well, we build each other up. However, what about the times when we fail to respond well to others? What happens when we speak hurtful or malicious words? Even in this situation, if the hearts of the two parties are not hardened, there is hope for recovering and building trust. When we tell our stories and interact together as brothers and sisters in Christ, we can err on both sides. The person telling the story may make statements that offend or hurt the listener, or the person listening may respond to a story in a disrespectful or patronizing manner. In both cases, the two must be willing to experience forgiveness. The one must be willing to own up to his or her error, whether that be willful malice or unintentional offensiveness. The other must be willing to respond with forgiveness.

When we confess and forgive, we weave new bonds of trust. When a bone that has been broken is properly set, it will heal to be stronger than it was before the injury. Even if one group member hurts another, trust can grow if both members go through a process of forgiveness. However, it may take time.

Forgiveness ought to distinguish Christian community from other groups. After all, we are the ones who have experienced the greatest forgiveness of all: reconciliation with our heavenly Father and all the blessing that accompanies it.

Conclusion

You will seek to go beyond surface community in the next session by sharing your life story with others. When you respond to those who share, be mindful of the need for edifying words over "honest" words, timeliness over assertiveness, and grace over judgment. And be willing to own any hurtful or offensive words that you speak, and seek forgiveness from those whom you wrong.

Assignment

Rehearse your "Life Story" presentation mentally or out loud. Prepare to be a good listener during others' "Life Story" presentations.

Life Story Presentations

You will now take a break from your normal sessions to share your "Life Story" presentations. You and the others in your group have done a lot of work to get to this point. This time could prove to be very significant in your life. Each person should make sure that the entire group does all it can to take advantage of the time spent presenting life stories. Enjoy these weeks with your group, and never lose sight of the Author of your story.

Session Aims

Presenter Aim: To clearly present your life story to the group members in order to invite them into your life as an exercise of trust leading to worship of God.

Listener Aim: To listen attentively to the life story in order to enter into the presenter's life for mutual encouragement and influence.

Preparation

Pray for the presenter throughout the week.

Show up to the group meeting on time.

Be ready to present or listen.

Content

The presentation time is serious and special for each person. You can count on the presenter being nervous about some of the content he or she will share and longing for the group's attention. Respect the presenter by being on time and listening attentively. Ask appropriate and thoughtful questions after the person is finished with his or her presentation.

Assignment

During the week following a group member's presentation, follow up with a brief note or phone call of encouragement.

Read *Session 7: Writing a Legacy*.

Writing a Legacy

The family you come from isn't as important as the family you're going to have.

—Ring Lardner, cited in *The Heritage*, Bruner and Ledbetter

It could be easy at this point to focus on your past and compare it to that of others. This may lead you to wonder what your future holds. What legacy will you leave in your own family? What legacy will you leave in your church and your community? Is there hope for leaving a godly legacy for those of the next generation?

In this session, you will examine the phrase "You have been handed a heritage but you will leave a legacy." Kurt D. Bruner and J. Otis Ledbetter address this issue in their book *The Heritage*.[1] This session will challenge you to consider what kind of heritage you will leave the next generation in your family, church, and community.

Session Aims

Individual Aim: To consider how to leave a godly heritage for those of the next generation.

Group Aim: To discuss how you can leave a godly heritage in others' lives.

Preparation

Read *Session 7: Writing a Legacy*.

Introduction

> *Children's children are a crown to the aged,*
> *and parents are the pride of their children.*
> *(Proverbs 17:6)*

Bruner and Ledbetter state,

> You cannot escape the ties of biology and identity that tie you to your parents and their parents, going back for generations. Your connections to preceding generations can bring the good or the bad. In turn, your connections to your children have a direct impact upon future generations for good or bad.[2]

Content

In the process of sharing your life story, you have undoubtedly seen the extraordinary influence of parents and other authority figures on children. No one has greater influence in a person's life than a parent or guardian. It will mark the person for a lifetime.

However, that influence does not determine how we live. We still make choices to live according to or contrary to those people's influence. In Ezekiel 18, God makes it clear that a person's heritage does not determine his or her destiny. Each individual has the chance either to ignore a godly heritage and live for self-glorification, or to oppose an ungodly heritage and endeavor to pursue godliness:

> *"But suppose this son has a son who sees all the sins his father commits, and though he sees them, he does not do such things:*
>
> > *"He does not eat at the mountain shrines*
> > > *or look to the idols of the house of Israel.*
> > *He does not defile his neighbor's wife.*
> > *He does not oppress anyone*
> > > *or require a pledge for a loan.*
> > *He does not commit robbery*
> > > *but gives his food to the hungry*
> > > *and provides clothing for the naked.*
> > *He withholds his hand from sin*
> > > *and takes no usury or excessive interest.*
> > *He keeps my laws and follows my decrees.*

He will not die for his father's sin; he will surely live. . . . The soul who sins is the one who will die. The son will not share the guilt of the father, nor will the father share the guilt of the son. The righteousness of the righteous man will be credited to him, and the wickedness of the wicked will be charged against him." (verses 14-17,20)

Everyone knows how destructive an ungodly heritage can be in someone's life. Television and movies are full of examples of this pattern. Men who were beaten by their fathers often beat their children. Women whose mothers married abusive men often marry abusive men. The cycle of pain and sin is a discouraging reality. However, a positive model for godliness can be just as powerful an influence as a negative one. Many of us have or will have children. Many of us currently have or will have influence in the lives of others who are not our children but are of a younger generation. The Scriptures portray the potential for this kind of influence:

> *He decreed statutes for Jacob*
> *   and established the law in Israel,*
> *which he commanded our forefathers*
> *   to teach their children,*
> *so the next generation would know them,*
> *   even the children yet to be born,*
> *   and they in turn would tell their children.*
> *Then they would put their trust in God*
> *   and would not forget his deeds*
> *   but would keep his commands.*
> *They would not be like their forefathers—*
> *   a stubborn and rebellious generation,*
> *whose hearts were not loyal to God,*
> *   whose spirits were not faithful to him.*
> *(Psalm 78:5-8)*

Of course, the hope of having a positive influence in others' lives, regardless of our heritage, doesn't ease the pain for those of us who have been handed a difficult heritage. We still feel deep loss. When exposed to others who have had a positive heritage, we can feel bitter when we compare our lives to theirs, as noted by Bruner and Ledbetter:

It just doesn't seem fair, does it? Some were given a wonderful, healthy positive heritage—a beautiful gown. Others were handed rags. Many of those who were given a solid heritage will find the process of passing on that tradition as natural as breathing. Others who received a very weak heritage will have no idea how to overcome the past, let alone create a positive future for the next generation. The good news is that both can create and give a wonderful heritage. Yes, the process of doing so will be much harder for some than others; but it can be done. It must be done. How? By reclaiming what you lost, or by learning to give what you didn't get.[3]

Our hope in Christ not only provides the way out of an ungodly heritage but also empowers us to establish a godly heritage. By walking with Christ, we can do what is against all odds, humanly speaking. As believers, we have the presence of God's Spirit to guide us to change, so the legacy we write in others' lives can be godly.

(For more on walking in the Spirit and the pursuit of godliness in the Christian life, see the *Integrity* study in this series.)

Conclusion

Bruner and Ledbetter write, "In evaluating your heritage it is important to understand and pass down the good aspect of what you were handed, break the cycle of hurt by leaving the bad behind, and to chart a new course as you build a new heritage for yourself and those you love."[4] Webster defines *heritage* as "something possessed as a result of one's natural situation or birth."[5] Bruner and Ledbetter define heritage in a similar way: "A heritage is the spiritual, emotional, and social legacy that is passed from parent to child . . . good or bad."[6]

We had no choice regarding our heritage—what values were instilled in us or how our parents treated us or each other. We received those values because God sovereignly placed us into particular family units. But we do have a choice in what we will leave to our friends and family. "Understanding the impact of our heritage is vital to the process of living. It can give you a new perspective on your past, a calm confidence in the present, and a meaningful sense of vision for your future."[7]

As you went through "Life Story," you all were brought face-to-face with your past—some with sadness, others with joy, and others somewhere in between. Now is the time to look at the different aspects of your heritage and plan how you can pass on a godly legacy to others.

Life Story

Introduction

> Now hear me relate
> My story, which perhaps thou hast not heard—
> Inviting thee to hear while I relate,
> Fond, were it not in hope of thy reply
>
> —John Milton, *Paradise Lost*

"Life Story" is a tool for redeemed pilgrims on a life journey. Along the way, relationships have been formed and lost, experiences enjoyed and endured. Yet God has chosen to use some of these relationships and experiences to help bring you to where you are today. "Life Story" will help you reflect on and discern what some of those formative relationships and experiences have been and how God has used them to mold and shape you.

The "Life Story" process will help you understand your uniqueness in Christ. "Life Story" goes beyond generalizations to highlight specific details of your life. "Life Story" will allow you to see your identity as it has developed in the particular relationships and experiences of your life.

"Life Story" will also help you tell your story to fellow travelers in a way that is creative, personal, organized, and focused on God. This aspect of "Life Story" will provide mutual encouragement as you see evidence of God's providence in your life. When you share your story, others will know and understand you in ways that draw you into a deeper experience of community. As you learn to share your life with others, you become a better member of a community.

Your responsibility in the "Life Story" process doesn't end when you prepare and present your story. You'll also hear others present their life stories, and you'll need to talk back and forth with them about their histories. As group members begin to grasp and appreciate one another's uniqueness, your community will grow in trust and authenticity.

This trust will lay the groundwork for deeper issues of character and holiness to surface. Trust is the community context that facilitates growth. (The *Integrity* study in this series addresses this kind of deeper growth.) Deeper intimacy will also draw affirmation from other group members about where you can serve others in the community. Gradually, you'll minister to others with your unique, God-given gifts for the utmost glory of Christ. (The *Ministry* study in this series will help you in this area.)

Benefits of "Life Story" include:
- Awareness of God's grace and providence
- Greater self-understanding
- Insight into how God works in different people's lives
- Deeper relationships
- Accountability
- Unconditional love and acceptance
- Deeper healing through openness
- Recognition of negative strongholds
- God's glory

Step A: Identifying the Chapters of Your Story

Divide your life into logical time sequences from birth to the present. You can divide your life into as many as seven sections, but you may find that your life divides best into fewer sections. The table below provides room to brainstorm two different life division schemes. Use the numbered spaces to write division titles for each time sequence. You may choose to divide your life into time sequences based on age, periods of school and work, geographic locations, or other arrangements you find appropriate. These divisions mark the various chapters of your story.

Life Division Scheme 1	Life Division Scheme 2
1.	1.
2.	2.
3.	3.
4.	4.
5.	5.
6.	6.
7.	7.

Once you've brainstormed two division schemes, choose the one that best reflects the divisions of your life. You have now chosen the major sections that will provide the basic structure of your story. Transfer the division titles to the "Experiences and Relationships" worksheets on the following pages. Use one worksheet page for each life division title. (Leave any extra worksheet pages blank.) Don't fill in your experiences and relationships yet, as you will do that when you complete Step B.

EXPERIENCES AND RELATIONSHIPS

Life division title:

My experiences and relationships during this time:

EXPERIENCES AND RELATIONSHIPS

Life division title:

My experiences and relationships during this time:

EXPERIENCES AND RELATIONSHIPS

Life division title:

My experiences and relationships during this time:

EXPERIENCES AND RELATIONSHIPS

Life division title:

My experiences and relationships during this time:

EXPERIENCES AND RELATIONSHIPS

Life division title:

My experiences and relationships during this time:

EXPERIENCES AND RELATIONSHIPS

Life division title:

My experiences and relationships during this time:

EXPERIENCES AND RELATIONSHIPS

Life division title:

My experiences and relationships during this time:

Step B: Identifying the Characters and Events of Your Story

Before we were aware of God's presence, He introduced people and events into our lives to draw us to Himself. However, we tend to believe that God didn't start authoring our lives until we believed in Christ. The basis of "Life Story" is the principle that nothing in our lives has happened apart from Him. In fact, He begins chapter one of a person's life story on the day of his or her conception (see Psalm 139:13-16).

How much of what God authors can we truly recognize? This question is legitimate because His plan for us is very broad. That which is not particularly striking to us now may prove to be very significant later in life, not to mention in eternity. And frankly, we often don't know why God allows certain experiences. He is indeed mysterious. Nevertheless, we can see God's hand at work. We are no different than the children of Israel, whom God admonished to remember Him and the works He performed on their behalf (see Exodus 13:3; Deuteronomy 4:9-14; 8:2; 15:15; Isaiah 46:9).

We should emulate David, who remembered God and His works (see Psalms 63:6-7; 77:11-12; 105:5; 143:5). David saw God's authorship in his life. His psalms are living expressions of a man who saw his life—his story—in the light of a sovereign and involved God. He wrote,

> *Where can I go from your Spirit?*
> *Where can I flee from your presence?*
> *If I go up to the heavens, you are there;*
> *if I make my bed in the depths, you are there.*
> *(Psalm 139:7-8)*

David concluded, "All the days ordained for me were written in your book before one of them came to be" (Psalm 139:16). Like David, we must see that the experiences and relationships of our lives come from God's hand and recognize and embrace the things God has done to bring us to where we are today.

You have already determined the chapter divisions of your story and trans-
ferred them to the "Experiences and Relationships" worksheets (pages 65-
71). Think through the experiences and relationships that correspond to
each life division, proceeding through this brainstorming process slowly
and methodically. As you do this exercise, you are finding an answer to the
fundamental question "What key relationships and experiences have made
up my life?" The following information on what we call the 4Hs (heritage,
heroes, high points, hard times) will help you answer this question.

> *heritage:* that which comes or belongs to one by reason of birth; an
> inherited lot or portion[1]

God's sovereignty is abundantly clear in the things you have through no
achievement of your own. A sobering thought is that "he himself gives all
men life and breath and everything else. From one man he made every
nation of men, that they should inhabit the whole earth; and he determined the times set for them and the exact places where they should live"
(Acts 17:25-26). When, where, why, and to whom you were born is significant. The resulting economic status, ethnicity, values, traditions, skills,
pleasures, and ways of functioning are important factors in your story.
Particular events and relationships have contributed to your heritage and
influenced who you are today.

Heritage involves the fundamental and seemingly ordinary elements of
your life. The contents of this category rarely appear striking or extraordinary. Your heritage may contain elements you would write off as mundane,
commonplace, or uneventful, but you may discover experiences and relationships of great significance. Some questions to ask as you think through
this category are:
• How have my parents or primary caregivers influenced me?
• What was the general atmosphere in my home as I grew up?
• How have my ethnicity and culture played an important role in my
  life?
• What have my peer relationships been like over the years? Why?
• How have geographical factors influenced me?

> *hero:* a person who, in the opinion of others, has heroic qualities or
> has performed a heroic act and is regarded as a model or ideal[2]

Heroes are people who make a distinctly positive impression on your life through words or actions. They can be nearly anyone: a parent, relative, neighbor, teacher, friend, or coach. Heroes also can be people you have never met, such as political leaders or historical figures. Somehow, heroes touch you in life-changing ways.

Heroes can come into your life at any time. A hero may be a person from your heritage (such as your mom, dad, or friend), a person you associate with a high point in your life (such as a teacher, coach, camp counselor, or political figure), or a person who helped you in a hard time (such as a relative or even an author). Some questions to ask as you think through this category are:

- Who has influenced me for good? How did they specifically do so?
- After whom would I like to model my life? Why?
- Who inspires me? Why?
- Who has shaped my character or direction in life? How? Why?

> *high points:* those periods or events that have a distinctly positive meaning in your life

High points are often the best and most fulfilling seasons or experiences of your life. These times might include winning a district championship, making the honor roll, receiving an award, going on a vacation, visiting a long-distance friend, having a year of peace in the home, enjoying two years at a great job, or getting married. Some questions to ask as you think through this category are:

- What accomplishments have brought me fulfillment or special recognition? How? Why?
- What events or people have brought me great joy?
- At what points in my life did I feel particularly good about life? Why?
- When have I made my greatest contributions to life or others? How?

> *hard times:* those seasons of life or relationships that have been particularly difficult or painful

Hard times might include divorce, the loss of a friend or relative, struggle with an addiction, times of abuse, a breakup with a boyfriend or girlfriend, a broken engagement, an injury or sickness, a period of loneliness, or a time of great pressure and anxiety. Some questions to ask as you think through this category are:

- What incidents in my life are hard to talk about with others? Why?
- Who or what has been a source of pain in my life? When? Why?
- Toward whom do I harbor anger or bitterness? Whom do I struggle to forgive? Why?
- What has brought me great disappointment? Why?
- Through what injustices have I had to suffer?
- To what addictions or abuse have I been exposed either in my own life or in the lives of others?

General Questions. These additional questions will further stimulate your brainstorming. Feel free to use your own questions as well. Remember, this story is your life story, and God has used many different means to bring you to where you are today.

- Who are the memorable people from your past? Why are they so?
- What have been the most influential experiences in your life?
- What life dreams have you had in your past?
- When you think of your parents, what memories come to mind?
- What do you remember about where you grew up?
- What are significant questions with which you have wrestled in your lifetime? What experiences triggered the questions?

Write down all your thoughts on the "Experiences and Relationships" worksheets (pages 65-71). The brainstorming and recording will take some time. You will probably find the greatest success by brainstorming at several different times during the week. Experiences and relationships may come to mind when you're least expecting it, so be ready to write them down. As you look back over the years of your life, pray that the Lord will help you remember the key elements that highlight God's authorship in your life.

Spiritual Discipline Exercise — Thanksgiving

Set aside some time to spend expressing thanksgiving to God for the ways in which He has authored your life. Read back through your list of experiences and relationships to recall that for which you are thankful. You also may express your thanksgiving by contacting persons from your past and telling them how God has used them in your life.

Step C: Discerning the Formative Elements of Your Story

You can most easily recognize God's authorship through the formative experiences and relationships He has brought into your life. Formative experiences and relationships are those that have molded and shaped you. Your task now is to discern what the most formative elements are from your "Experiences and Relationships" worksheets.

First, transfer the division titles to the "Life Story Chapters" worksheets beginning on page 86. Then, distinguish those experiences and relationships that have had lasting effects from those that came and went. Many parts of life have been fun and even memorable, but you must focus on those that have been formative (affected you significantly). Transfer only your formative experiences and relationships to the appropriate spots on your "Life Story Chapters" worksheets.

Next, you will categorize each formative experience or relationship. The following three sections define the labels you will be using. It would be helpful to read all three sections before beginning the labeling process.

Recognizing Meaning and Purpose in Your Story

For each formative experience or relationship, use the following questions to try to determine the meaning and purpose behind each one:
- How has the experience or relationship shaped me (my attitudes, perspectives, habits, or values)?
- What primary lesson have I retained from the experience or relationship?
- How did the experience or relationship affect my view of God? My view of people?
- Why did God bring it into my life?
- Where has it led me?
- What consequences—good or bad—came from it?

Write **MP** (**M**eaning and **P**urpose) beside any formative experiences and relationships for which you understand the significant meanings and purposes for your story. Jot down a note to help you remember the meaning and purpose you currently attach to the experience or relationship. Keep in mind, though, that certain formative experiences or relationships may not lend themselves to reasonable explanations of why God brought them into your life. You may have great difficulty discerning the meaning and purpose behind certain events. The following section addresses this issue.

Recognizing Faith Points in Your Story

Working through the "Life Story" process is an exercise of faith. You need faith at several levels. First, you need faith to say that God's work in your life has an overarching plot and that He wants you to reflect on it and grow in appreciating His providence. You need to believe the time invested in prayer, reflection, and writing is well worth the discoveries you will make.

You also need faith to move on with your story when you don't understand various elements in the plots. You may not be able to discern the meaning and purpose of some formative experiences and relationships. This difficulty is okay. Those experiences and relationships are "faith points." Though you cannot discern their meaning now, you choose to move on in faith, believing that God's sovereign work is trustworthy and His nature is good. Because you are looking at stories not yet complete, the faith points may eventually make sense as your story unfolds. Marshall Shelley, editor of *Leadership* magazine, said the following about God's authorship in his life after he lost two children:

> Even as a child, I loved to read, and I quickly learned that I would most likely be confused during the opening chapters of a novel. New characters were introduced. Disparate, seemingly random events took place. Subplots were complicated and didn't seem to make any sense in relation to the main plot. But I learned to keep reading. Why? Because you know that the author, if he or she is good, will weave them all together by the end of the book. Eventually each element will be meaningful.[3]

Eugene Peterson offers a similar reflection:

> I'm living in a plot with characters, and all the stuff connects in
> some way or another. What happens today—even though I don't
> understand it and it doesn't make any sense—is going to make
> sense thirty chapters down the road.[4]

Your faith points may gain clarity in meaning and purpose as you patiently
live out your story. However, some experiences and relationships may
remain faith points throughout life. You may have to carry certain injustices, tragedies, and pains in faith forever without explanation. Although
you may recognize some good from them, link certain outcomes in life to
them, or find that ministry stems from them, the events may always be
unanswered mysteries under God's sovereignty.

The life of Job provides an example. Job lost all of his oxen, donkeys,
sheep, camels, servants, and children (see Job 1:13-19). This tremendous
tragedy was obviously a faith point in Job's life. In the following forty-
one chapters, Job never found an answer for "all the trouble the LORD
had brought upon him" (Job 42:11). Why did God allow this tragedy to
happen? Job didn't know. What Job took away from this experience was
that he didn't have to ascribe purpose to it. From this formative experience, he walked away in humble faith. God did bless him twofold for all
he lost, but this blessing was in no way the meaning for the loss. Yes,
good came from the experience, but the experience remained a tragic
evil that rested in the mystery of God. You may rather not admit this
reality, but you may find that some events fall into this category in your
own life.

Where you cannot find meaning and purpose, you must find faith! Write
FP (Faith Point) beside any formative experiences and relationships that
are faith points for you. At this time in the exercise, each of your formative experiences and relationships should be labeled either **MP** or **FP**.

Recognizing God's Faithfulness in Your Story

As you evaluate the experiences and relationships of your life, God's faithfulness should be more than evident. You need to recognize the events that
demonstrate God's faithfulness and set them up as pillars for further

reflection in the future. After the Israelites crossed the Jordan River and entered the Promised Land, God instructed them to set up a heap of stones from the river as a memorial for their descendants forever (see Joshua 4). You should set up the distinct events of your past that demonstrate God's faithfulness as memorials for you, your children, and others. These memorials may serve as anchors for your faith in the future.

Write **STONE** (memorial Stone) beside any formative experiences and relationships that serve as memorials to God's faithfulness. This word **STONE** is in addition to the label of **MP** or **FP** that you have already given each formative experience and relationship.

Step D: Learning About the Author and Main Character of Your Story

Once you have determined the formative experiences and relationships in your life, reflect on what you have learned from them about God and yourself. As you pray and meditate on each formative event, ask yourself the following questions:

1. As the Author of my life, what has God revealed about *Himself* through this relationship or experience?

   • His attributes

   • His character

   • His works

2. What has God revealed about *me*, the main character of my life, through this relationship or experience?

- My temperament

- My strengths

- My weaknesses

- My values

Use the answers that come to mind to fill in the "What I learn about God" and "What I learn about myself" sections of your "Life Story Chapters" worksheets (pages 86-92).

Spiritual Discipline Exercise — Meditation

Spend some time reflecting on and looking up Bible verses that have had a significant influence on your life. Meditate on those verses and how God has used them to shape your view of Him, yourself, and the world. Note the verses and any thoughts about them below.

Step E: Identifying Themes in Your Story

Now that you have gained significant understanding of the elements of your story as well as insight into God and yourself, ask yourself, *How do the different parts of my life relate to one another?* As you think of how various people, events, and lessons relate, you will discover the themes of your life story. In a work of literature, the theme is what the author seeks to communicate. The theme answers the question "What is this story about?"

After considerable reflection, write down several themes that emerge from your life on the "Themes" worksheet on page 93. Identifying themes will help you effectively evaluate and articulate your story.

Spiritual Discipline Exercise — Evangelism

Pray for and commit to sharing your life themes with at least one friend who isn't a Christian. As you share your themes, be attentive to opportunities to explain the gospel of Christ to him or her. Use the space below to write down the name of at least one nonbeliever with whom you will commit to sharing your life themes.

Step F: Assigning Chapter Titles to Your Story

Based on what you have uncovered thus far, create chapter titles for each of the chapters of your story. You already have life division titles that explain each division straightforwardly ("College Years," for example), but the chapter titles capture the flow and meaning of your story ("Out of the Nest," for instance). Chapter titles are more descriptive. Be creative, and if you have a predominant metaphor, connect the titles to your metaphor. For example, if your metaphor is one of a journey, you might label your chapters "Preparation," "Setting Out," and "Encountering Obstacles." Write your chapter titles on the "Life Story Chapters" worksheets beginning on the next page.

LIFE STORY CHAPTERS

Chapter title:

Life division title:

My formative experiences and relationships during this time:

What I learned about God: | **What I learned about myself:**

LIFE STORY CHAPTERS

Chapter title:

Life division title:

My formative experiences and relationships during this time:

What I learned about God:

What I learned about myself:

LIFE STORY CHAPTERS

Chapter title:

Life division title:

My formative experiences and relationships during this time:

What I learned about God:

What I learned about myself:

LIFE STORY CHAPTERS

Chapter title:

Life division title:

My formative experiences and relationships during this time:

What I learned about God:

What I learned about myself:

LIFE STORY CHAPTERS

Chapter title:

Life division title:

My formative experiences and relationships during this time:

What I learned about God:

What I learned about myself:

LIFE STORY CHAPTERS

Chapter title:

Life division title:

My formative experiences and relationships during this time:

What I learned about God: **What I learned about myself:**

LIFE STORY CHAPTERS

Chapter title:

Life division title:

My formative experiences and relationships during this time:

What I learned about God:

What I learned about myself:

THEMES

The themes of my story:

Theme A

Theme B

Theme C

Step G: Creatively Preparing Your Story

You will now plan how to creatively communicate your life story by using images to help the listeners see and understand it. One way to use images is to look for a *dominant metaphor*. A metaphor is an image used to make a comparison for descriptive purposes. You could describe your life as a hike up a barren mountain. You could describe yourself as a student always struggling to win an A+ grade. You could say you spent the first half of your life falling deeper into a spiritual sickness and the second half getting progressively well. These are all metaphors.

Your themes and chapter titles may suggest a metaphor. For instance, one of your themes may be "Pursuing confidence through recognition from authority figures." A possible metaphor that emerges from that theme is "A student driven to get an A+." Note that this picture of a student diligently studying for the top grade could also be a metaphor for a theme of "Seeking popularity at all costs" or "Doing whatever it takes to obtain wealth."

The connection between metaphor and theme is very important. The metaphor communicates the theme vividly with a strong mental picture. So if your life naturally surfaces a metaphor that communicates its major themes, then develop and use the metaphor. However, your goal is not to come up with a dazzling metaphor; your goal is to communicate your story effectively.

Some people find it extremely hard to encapsulate their lives within a single metaphor. If you have this difficulty, look instead for *illustrative material*. Think through images from the world of sports, literature, mechanics, the arts, or nature. Consider using drawings, personal photographs, magazine cutouts, computer graphics, and even old video clips or family movies to animate your story. You might choose to include music or poetry to enhance your story.

For example, one could use a briefcase filled with various contents as an illustrative way to tell the story. Someone else may use his skill in painting watercolors to present his story to the group. Another person may make a collage or a photograph album. Be creative, but remain concise. You have a limited amount of time to present your story to the group. This time will pass quickly.

As you work on the creative expression of your story, keep these questions in mind:

- Can I present my story within the allotted time?
- Do my chapter titles reflect the content of each life division? Can I explain why I chose the titles I did?
- Can I make a clear connection from chapter to chapter? Does my story flow?
- How does the metaphor and/or illustrative material enhance my message?

By the end of this step, you should have a clear and tangible presentation of your life story in hand. You will tell your own story as God has authored it, so tell it honestly and tell it well.

Leader's Guide

Introduction

This leader's guide will:
- Explain the intended purpose of each session and how each session fits into the entire study
- Provide you with plenty of discussion questions so that you can choose a few that suit your group
- Suggest other ways of interacting over the material

The first step in leading this study is to read "A Model of Spiritual Transformation" beginning on page 9. The section describes three broad approaches to growth and explains how the four studies in the series fit together.

There's more involved in leading a small group, however, than just understanding the study and its objective. The main skill you'll need is creating a group environment that facilitates authentic interaction among people. Every leader does this in his or her own style, but here are two principles necessary for all:

1. *Avoid the temptation to speak whenever people don't immediately respond to one of your questions.* As the leader, you may feel pressure to break the silence. Often, though, leaders overestimate how much silence has gone by. Several seconds of silence may seem like a minute to the leader. However, usually people just need time to collect their thoughts before they respond. If you wait patiently for their responses, they will usually take that to mean you really do want them to say what they think. On the other hand, if you consistently break the silence yourself, they may not feel the need to speak up.

2. *Avoid being a problem solver.* If you immediately try to solve every problem that group members voice, they won't feel comfortable sharing issues of personal struggle. Why? Because most people, when sharing their problems, initially want to receive acceptance

and empathy rather than advice. They want others to understand and care about the troubled state of their soul. Giving immediate advice can often communicate that you feel they are not bright enough to figure out the solution.

Getting a Small Group Started

You may be gathering a group of friends to do a study together or possibly you've volunteered to lead a group that your church is assembling. Regardless of the circumstances, God has identified you as the leader.

You are probably a peer of the other group members. Some may have read more theology than you, some may have more church ministry experience than you, and yet God has providentially chosen you as the leader. You're not the "teacher" or the sole possessor of wisdom—you are simply responsible to create an atmosphere that facilitates genuine interaction.

One of the most effective ways you can serve your group is to *make clear what is expected*. You are the person who informs group members. They need to know, for example, where and when your first meeting will be held. If you're meeting in a home and members need maps, make sure they receive them in a timely manner. If members don't have study books, help them each obtain one. To create a hospitable setting for your meetings, you will need to plan for refreshments or delegate that responsibility to others. A group phone and e-mail list may also be helpful; ask the group if it's okay to distribute their contact information to one another. Make sure there's a sense of order. You may even want to chart out a tentative schedule of all the sessions, including any off weeks for holidays.

The first several sessions are particularly important because they are when you will communicate your vision for the group. You'll want to explain your vision several times during your first several meetings. Many people need to hear it several times before it really sinks in, and some will probably miss the first meeting or two. Communicate your vision and expectations concisely so that plenty of time remains for group discussion. People will drop out if the first session feels like a monologue from the leader.

Ideally, you'll have done the *Identity* study in this series together, so you'll already know quite a bit about each other. But if your group is brand new and starting with *Community*, it will be helpful to spend one full meeting building rapport before diving into the material. One valuable thing to do in this first meeting is to let group members tell a brief history of themselves. This could involve a handful of facts about where they come from and how they ended up in this group. This brief history will be like a taste of the "Life Story" exercise that will culminate this study.

Also, in your first or second meeting, ask group members to share their expectations. The discussion may take the greater part of a meeting, but it's worth the time invested because it will help you understand each person's perspective. Here are some questions for initiating a discussion of group members' expectations:

- How well do you expect to get to know others in the group?
- Describe your previous experiences with small groups. Do you expect this group to be similar or different?
- What do you hope the group will be like by the time the study ends?
- How do you think this group will contribute to your walk with Christ?
- Do you need to finish the meeting by a certain time, or do you prefer open-ended meetings? Do you expect to complete this study in ten sessions, or will you be happy extending it by a few sessions if the additional time serves your other goals for the group?

The "Life Story" exercise in this study is time-consuming, so be sure to discuss expectations about it. You might page through it together and estimate how much time people will spend at home working on their stories. Some will want to invest more time than others, and that's fine; everyone will get out of it what he or she puts in. But if some strongly resist the idea of investing hours in a presentation of their life stories, it will be helpful to discuss that up front. You may need to encourage some members who resist the idea of making a long presentation. There will be plenty of time beforehand to discuss fears about speaking to a group, and no one will be forced to do it.

"Life Story" will also require extensive group time. As you'll see on page 103, you may need several group meetings or an all-day Saturday retreat to allow everyone time to tell a story and receive the group's feedback. Sixty to ninety minutes per life story should be adequate. Is the group prepared to devote seven meetings plus a Saturday, or some other arrangement? As the leader, you should come to this first meeting prepared to suggest a scenario that you think will work for your group. You should also come prepared to be flexible if others have alternate suggestions.

If you have an extended discussion of people's expectations, you probably won't actually begin session 1 of this study guide until the second time you meet. This is more likely if your group is just forming than if your group has been together for some time. By the time you start the first session in the study guide, group members ought to be accustomed to interacting with one another. This early investment will pay big dividends. If you plan to take a whole meeting (or even two) to lay this kind of groundwork, be sure to tell the group what you're doing and why. Otherwise, some people may think you're simply inefficient and unable to keep the group moving forward.

Remember that many people will feel nervous during the first meeting. This is natural; don't feel threatened by it. Your attitude and demeanor will set the tone. If you are passive, the group will lack direction and vision. If you are all business and no play, they will expect that the group will have a formal atmosphere, and you will struggle to get people to lighten up. If you are all play and no business, they will expect the group to be all fluff and won't take it seriously. Allow the group some time and freedom to form a "personality." If many group members enjoy a certain activity, join in with them. Don't try to conform the group to your interests. You may have to be willing to explore new activities.

What does the group need from you initially as the leader?

- *Approachability:* Be friendly, ask questions, avoid dominating the discussion, engage with group members before and after the sessions, allow group members opportunities to ask you questions too.

- *Connections:* Pay attention to how you can facilitate bonding. (For example, if you learn in separate conversations that two group members, Joe and Tom, went to State University, you might say, "Joe, did you know that Tom also went to State U?")

- *Communication of Logistics:* Be simple, clear, and concise. (For instance, be clear about what will be involved in the group sessions, how long they will last, and where and when they will occur.)

- *Summary of Your Leadership Style:* You might want to put together some thoughts about your style of leadership and be prepared to share them with the group. You might include such issues as:

1. The degree of flexibility with which you operate (for example, your willingness to go on "rabbit trails" versus staying on topic)

2. Your level of commitment to having prayer or worship as a part of the group

3. Your attentiveness, or lack thereof, to logistics (making sure to discuss the details surrounding your group, such as when and where you are meeting, or how to maintain communication with one another if something comes up)

4. The degree to which you wear your emotions on your sleeve

5. Any aspects of your personality that have often been misunderstood (for instance, "People sometimes think that I'm not interested in what they are saying because I don't immediately respond, when really I'm just pondering what they were saying.")

6. Any weaknesses you are aware of as a leader (for example, "Because I can tend to dominate the group by talking too much, I will appreciate anybody letting me know if I am doing so." Or, "I get very engaged in discussion and can consequently lose track of time, so I may need you to help me keep on task so we finish on time.")

7. How you plan to address any concerns you have with group members (for instance, "If I have concerns about the way anyone is interacting in the group, perhaps by consistently offending another group member, I will set up time to get together and address it with that person face-to-face.")

- *People Development:* Allow group members to exercise their spiritual gifts. See their development not as a threat to your leadership but as a sign of your success as a leader. For instance, if group members enjoy worshiping together and you have someone who can lead the group in worship, encourage that person to do so. However, give direction in this so that the person knows exactly what you expect. Make sure he or she understands how much worship time you want.

Beginning the Sessions

Before you jump into session 1, make sure that group members have had a chance to read "A Model of Spiritual Formation" beginning on page 9 and "A Method for the Biblical Exercise" beginning on page 17. Also, ask if they have done what is listed in the "Preparation" section of session 1. Emphasize that the assignments for each session are as important as the group meetings and that inadequate preparation for a session diminishes the whole group's experience.

Overview of *Community*

This study focuses on two objectives. First, it exposes group members to principles that build authentic Christian community. Second, it guides the group to experience deeper community through a tool called "Life Story." This tool helps group members put together a presentation of their lives that they share with the group.

Because "Life Story" is such a focus of the study, the group can tend to see the sessions merely as steps leading up to the "Life Story" presentations. The sessions do prepare group members for the "Life Story" presentations, but they do more than that. They also expose group members to principles of Christian community. In your session discussions, you'll want to emphasize how important the principles are to genuine community.

The Order of Sessions

The first few sessions will address why believers need to identify the significance of their experiences rather than just the facts. How did that experience affect me? How did it affect others? Then the study will focus on listening, encouragement, counsel, and forgiveness. The next several sessions will then revolve around "Life Story" presentations. Finally, after the presentations there is one additional session that wraps up the study. This session encourages group members to consider how they can positively contribute to others' life stories, building a godly heritage within their sphere of influence.

Life Story Presentations

There are various ways to do "Life Story" presentations, depending on the number of people in your group. If you have five or fewer members, you may continue with your normal schedule, doing one "Life Story" presentation per week. Your group will need to clarify the expected time for sharing your stories. A typical scenario is to give forty minutes for the presentation and ten to fifteen minutes for audience response and questions afterward.

If you have more than five people, you should consider doing an overnight retreat or spending a Saturday together in order to hear several presentations at once.

Discussion Questions

This "Leader's Guide" contains questions that we think will help you attain the goal of each session and build community in your group. Use our discussion questions in addition to the ones you come up with on your own, but don't feel pressured to use all of them. However, we think it's wise to use some of them. If one question is not a good vehicle for discussion, then use another. It can be helpful to rephrase the questions in your own words.

Session 1: God's Authorship

This session introduces the concept of story in group members' lives. They are encouraged to think of their lives as a narrative that God has authored. God's authorship raises the issues of divine sovereignty and human free will. You'll need to observe your group members' thoughts about God's sovereignty and human free will. Some people will resist the idea that both are true. Remember that the goal of this session is not to resolve the tension; rather, it is to acknowledge that it remains a mystery.

Use the following questions to help group members think through how they currently view God's authorship in their lives. The questions will unearth important information about how group members regard their past, as well as the decisions they are currently making.

1. Have you ever thought of your life as a story?

2. If so, in what genre would you classify your story (romance, tragedy, epic, comedy)?

3. Does your understanding of life lean more toward God's sovereignty or man's responsibility? Explain.

4. How will your answer to the previous question affect the way you work through "Life Story"?

5. Based on the reading and our discussion so far, how do you think "Life Story" will help you better understand yourself and God?

6. How do you think it will build trust among group members?

Spend some time in prayer for the process through which the Lord will lead your group. Explain the assignment for next week. Although the group members should have read "Life Story: Step A," you should turn to that section to make sure they understand how to break their lives down into logical divisions. Encourage the group to start praying now about the "Life Story" process. Pray that God will open eyes, hearts, and minds as members go through their stories in this study.

Session 2: Experiences and Relationships

Ask if each member completed his or her life divisions and if anyone has questions about that step in the process. Find out if anyone had difficulty finding logical divisions, and help those who did have difficulty.

Use the following questions to establish the importance of looking back over one's past:

1. What are the two extreme views regarding the utilization of past events in our present experiences?

2. In your opinion, does this session adequately present the proper biblical perspective on the past? Why, or why not?

3. How do you think you can use what you learned about your past experiences and relationships to glorify God as Paul did?

4. Can this be true even if your experiences are not as dramatic as Paul's? How so?

Take the next fifteen to twenty minutes to review "Life Story: Step B." Make sure each group member understands what to accomplish during the following week. Go through the 4Hs, which will help people brainstorm their many experiences and relationships. You must understand Step B well in order to lead your group through it.

Session 3: Formative Elements and Themes

Ask if each member made a thorough list of experiences and relationships for the divisions of his or her life. Ask if anyone has questions concerning that step in the process. Discuss as necessary. As the leader, you may want to bring one of your "Experiences and Relationships" worksheets to show to the group as an example.

Themes are hard for many people to grasp. Keep people from thinking in terms of theme until they finish the process of identifying the most formative elements in their lives. After that, when they skim back over their findings, a few themes should emerge as issues they have faced consistently. Here are some suggested questions:

1. Can you discern the similarities and differences between the three categories listed for formative experiences and relationships? (That is, experiences that seem meaningful, faith points in which you have to trust God that there's meaning in a painful experience, and pillars of faithfulness.)

2. Can you distinguish between themes and metaphors?

3. Can you see God's hand in the details of some of your experiences? What about in the broad sweep of your life?

4. How can looking for God in these two levels—the details and the broad sweep—change your perspective or your lifestyle?

Pray with your group about the next steps in the "Life Story" process. Ask God for wisdom as the group members seek to determine what events and relationships have had lasting effects on their lives.

Session 4: The Art of Speech

The following questions will help you understand how much public speaking experience group members have had, discover what barriers may inhibit them from truly benefiting from their "Life Story" experiences, and open avenues through which you can encourage group members in the presentations of their stories.

1. What public speaking experiences have you had in the past? In what kinds of settings did they take place?

2. What are some fears you have experienced in speaking before groups of people?

3. As you consider sharing your story with this group, what fears do you have?

4. What can the group begin doing today that will help alleviate those fears?

5. Of the various insecurities mentioned in the session, which will most likely affect you?

6. What can you do to avoid the insecurities? What can the group do to help you?

7. Do you think you can present your life story adequately in the allotted time? Why or why not?

8. How might someone make a story inviting? Influential?

9. How can the use of a metaphor make your story inviting and influential? (See "Life Story: Step G.")

Leave a few minutes at the end of your time to address any questions group members may have concerning the "Life Story" process. They have completed their formative experiences and relationships sections and will work on what they have learned about God and themselves for the next session. Make sure they understand that they will present their stories to the group. Clarify what the allotted time will be. (We suggest at least forty-five minutes for the presentation and at least fifteen minutes for the group's feedback. More time is preferable.) Also, tell them that questions and prayer will follow each presentation.

Session 5: Listening

Lead the group in one of the following exercises:

Recent Personal Conversation

Have group members identify and think about a significant conversation they have had recently. Lead them through an examination of it as follows:

> Think of a recent conversation in which a friend shared something personal with you. Write down some details from that conversation. Record the details of what the person said, to the best of your memory. Record the nonverbal forms of communication that he or she expressed. For example, if your friend was visibly discouraged, write that down. If he or she was overjoyed, make note of it. Take a few minutes to recollect as much about that interaction as you can.

Illustration Conversation

Tell the group a story from your own life of a recent significant conversation. It might be something like this:

> "Last night I received a phone call from a very close friend. He called to tell me that he was accepted to graduate school. His voice was filled with excitement, as if he could hardly wait to share his good news. He seemed to want to share the joy he was experiencing. I was aware of his application, and we had previously spoken of how great the opportunity would be if he got accepted but also of how I would miss his friendship if he went off to graduate school. My response was, 'That's terrific! I mean, that's too bad—I'm just kidding.' I asked him how he was feeling when he heard and who had informed him of his acceptance. He shared that the professor who was sponsoring him had called. I was so thrilled to share the excitement of the moment with him! The short conversation affirmed to me the value he placed on our relationship."

Movie Clip

Play a short segment from a movie of someone sharing a very personal story of something that happened to him or her. Then analyze how well people in the group could pick up on the verbal and nonverbal communication.

After you do one of the three listening exercises, discuss some of the following questions. You may have to adjust the questions to fit the particular exercise you chose.

1. What were the facts your friend shared with you?

2. What, if any, emotions accompanied those facts? What helped you identify the emotions?

3. What was the main point of the story?

4. What follow-up questions did you ask or do you wish you had asked?

5. What insights did you gain about the storyteller?

6. What forms of nonverbal communication did the storyteller use?

7. Why is nonverbal communication more believable than verbal?

Here are some suggested questions to help prepare group members for the "Life Story" presentations. The main point of this session is to get them thinking about how crucial listening is for building a sense of community. For instance, if group members don't listen well, they will be limited in their ability to give a loving response to the presenter.

1. In light of the information in the session, why do we emphasize expressing our stories creatively during the presentation time?

2. Why is it important to limit our presentations to the allotted time?

3. What signal do we communicate by showing up late to someone's story?

4. What are some of the positive and negative signals listeners might give as someone presents his or her story?

5. When we have listened attentively enough to ask a good follow-up question, what does that question communicate to the person telling

the story? (A sample follow-up question is, "You mentioned that you have a history of not getting along with your sister. Why is that?")

6. How does it make you feel when you are beginning to share something very personal with someone and he or she is distracted? (For instance, you notice that he or she is looking attentively at someone over your shoulder.)

Session 6: Encouragement, Counsel, and Forgiveness

Read through the following material and become familiar with the content. This topic is crucial, so be ready to make the most of this session. If you really want to learn more about encouragement, you might want to obtain a copy of *Encouragement: The Key to Caring*, by Larry Crabb and Dan Allender.[1]

This session will bring about a lot of discussion and sharing, so use your time well. Begin the session by jumping right into the necessity of responding well when others share significant and personal stories.

After a group member shares his or her life story, the others should respond during the following week with a brief note or phone call of encouragement. A note can be typed in e-mail, handwritten on a card, or in any form the listener feels is appropriate. The primary purpose of the communication is to offer encouragement to the presenter. Or, if a part of someone's story particularly touched you, you can call the person and tell him or her directly. If something the storyteller said challenged you, explain what it was and thank the person. If you feel the person has demonstrated courage in an area of life, affirm him or her for this courage. If you are thankful for what God has done in or through the person, let him or her know how you are thankful. Use the following questions to help spark discussion about this section:

1. When you share something personal with someone, what do you want most in response from that person?

2. As you prepare to share your story, what are some of your fears? How can Crabb and Allender's first principle of encouragement help us settle each other's fears?

3. What do you think about Crabb and Allender's second principle of encouragement that "understanding is sometimes better than advice"? Can you give an example from your life when this was true?

4. Crabb and Allender's third principle is "Words that encourage take into account both the need for relationship and the need for meaning." What does this statement mean to you?

5. In what way does inattentive listening affect a person's ability to encourage?

6. How does it make you feel when someone does not listen to you with his or her full attention? How does it affect the level of vulnerability you express?

7. In the gospel accounts, how did Christ demonstrate attentiveness to others? Can you give examples?

Conclude this session by praying for God to offer both encouragement and spiritual direction to each group member over the future weeks of sharing stories. Address any questions about "Life Story." Make sure that group members know when they will be presenting their stories and that next week's presenters are ready. Reemphasize how important it is not to miss anyone's presentation. If, however, group members must miss a "Life Story" presentation, it is ideal for them to get some time with the presenter and hear at least a summary of the story.

Life Story Presentations

We ask a lot from people when we have them share their stories. Even if the group is laughing and in a great mood, you can count on the presenter being nervous or even worried. As the leader, it is your job to set the right atmosphere from the start. Make sure that you and all group members are respectful and listen attentively during each presentation. Start on time and help the presenter end on time.

The following is a suggested flow for these presentation group times:
- Opening prayer for the presenter
- "Life Story" presentation
- Questions and comments
- Group prayer and thanksgiving for the presenter
- Group members are reminded to write notes of encouragement during the week

Session 7: Writing a Legacy

This session is designed to wrap up the experience of "Life Story" presentations and provide a transition into the *Integrity* study. It points group members toward the issues of growth, holiness, and service. Though we all carry scars with us through life, we can rejoice because there is hope for redemption in this life as well as in the next. The following questions will help you lead this discussion:

1. What specific aspects of your heritage do you feel you must oppose in order for you to leave a godly heritage to others?

2. What do you think were the weaknesses of your parents in their raising of you? In what ways do you want to differ from them in the way you parent?

3. What do you think were the strengths of your parents or guardians in their raising of you? How difficult do you anticipate it will be to follow their example with your own children?

4. If you don't have children and don't anticipate having any in the future, how do you think you might have a positive impact on the heritage of someone from the next generation?

5. How would you want someone of the next generation to describe his or her relationship with you twenty to forty years from now?

Conclusion

We hope this study has been helpful for you and your group members. We desire to provide materials that help believers grow in Christ through small-group communities. Don't hesitate to contact us if you have any questions!

Phone: (214) 841-3515
E-mail: sf@dts.edu

Notes

A Method for the Biblical Exercise

1. Howard G. Hendricks and William D. Hendricks, *Living By the Book* (Chicago: Moody, 1991), p. 166.

Session 1: God's Authorship

1. D. A. Carson, "God's Love and God's Sovereignty," *Bibliotheca Sacra* (July–September 1999), p. 263.
2. Carson, p. 264.

Session 3: Formative Elements and Themes

1. "formative," *Webster's Encyclopedic Unabridged Dictionary of the English Language* (New York: Gramercy Books, 1996), p. 557.
2. "meaning," *Webster's Encyclopedic Unabridged Dictionary of the English Language* (New York: Gramercy Books, 1996), p. 888.
3. "purpose," *Webster's Encyclopedic Unabridged Dictionary of the English Language* (New York: Gramercy Books, 1996), p. 1167.
4. "theme," Kathleen Morner and Ralph Rausch, *NTC's Dictionary of Literary Terms* (Lincolnwood, Ill.: National Textbook, 1996), p. 223.

Session 4: The Art of Speech

1. Donald K. Smith, *Creating Understanding: A Handbook for Christian Communication Across Cultural Landscapes* (Grand Rapids, Mich.: Zondervan, 1992), p. 29.
2. Smith, p. 39.
3. Haddon Robinson, *Biblical Preaching: The Development and Delivery of Expository Messages* (Grand Rapids, Mich.: Baker, 1980), p. 38.
4. Friedrich Nietzsche, quoted in Duane Litfin, *Public Speaking: A Handbook for Christians*, 2nd ed. (Grand Rapids, Mich.: Baker, 1992), p. 280.
5. Smith, p. 40.

Session 6: Encouragement, Counsel, and Forgiveness

1. Larry Crabb and Dan Allender, *Encouragement: The Key to Caring* (Grand Rapids, Mich.: Zondervan, 1984), pp. 28-30.
2. Crabb and Allender, p. 28.
3. Crabb and Allender, p. 104. The three principles of encouragement are taken from *Encouragement: The Key to Caring* by Larry Crabb and Dan Allender. Copyright © 1984. Used by permission of Zondervan.
4. Crabb and Allender, p. 106.
5. Crabb and Allender, p. 107.

Session 7: Writing a Legacy

1. Kurt D. Bruner and Otis J. Ledbetter, *The Heritage: Giving and Receiving an Inheritance of Love* (Chicago: Moody, 1996), p. 11.
2. Bruner and Ledbetter, p. 14.
3. Bruner and Ledbetter, p. 15.
4. "heritage," *Webster's Ninth New Collegiate Dictionary* (Springfield, Ill.: Merriam-Webster, 1985), p. 566.
5. Bruner and Ledbetter, p. 27.
6. Bruner and Ledbetter, p. 31.
7. Bruner and Ledbetter, p. 31.

Life Story

1. "heritage," *Webster's Encyclopedic Unabridged Dictionary of the English Language* (New York: Gramercy Books, 1996), p. 664.
2. "hero," *Webster's Encyclopedic Unabridged Dictionary of the English Language* (New York: Gramercy Books, 1996), p. 665.
3. Marshall Shelley, *Leadership* xvii, no. 4 (fall 1996), pp. 89-90.
4. Eugene Peterson, interview by Sandra Glahn, in "What's Your Story?" *The Threshing Floor* (Dallas Theological Seminary: Dallas, March 1997).

Leader's Guide

1. Larry Crabb and Dan Allender, *Encouragement: The Key to Caring* (Grand Rapids, Mich.: Zondervan, 1984).

OTHER BOOKS IN THE TRANSFORMING LIFE SERIES.

Identity

Pinpoint key elements of who you are—your heritage, roles, and distinctiveness—in Christ.
1-57683-558-8

Integrity

Identify ways to overcome the habits that are contrary to the values you profess as a Christian. Instead discover Christlike character traits you can develop and live out.
1-57683-561-8

Ministry

Your interests, struggles, and talents can help you discern how God has uniquely designed you to serve. This study will help you find your unique niche in the body of Christ.
1-57683-562-6

To get your copies, visit your local bookstore, call 1-800-366-7788, or log on to www.navpress.com. Ask for a FREE catalog of NavPress products. Offer BPA.